William Shakespeare's

Titus Andronicus
In Plain and Simple English

BookCaps Study Guides
www.bookcaps.com

Table of Contents:

About This Series

The "Classic Retold" series started as a way of telling classics for the modern reader—being careful to preserve the themes and integrity of the original. Whether you want to understand Shakespeare a little more or are trying to get a better grasps of the Greek classics, there is a book waiting for you!

Characters

SATURNINUS, son to the late Emperor of Rome, afterwards Emperor

BASSIANUS, brother to Saturninus

TITUS ANDRONICUS, a noble Roman

MARCUS ANDRONICUS, Tribune of the People, and brother to Titus

Sons to Titus Andronicus:
LUCIUS
QUINTUS
MARTIUS
MUTIUS

YOUNG LUCIUS, a boy, son to Lucius

PUBLIUS, son to Marcus Andronicus

Kinsmen to Titus:
SEMPRONIUS
CAIUS
VALENTINE

AEMILIUS, a noble Roman

Sons to Tamora:
ALARBUS
DEMETRIUS
CHIRON

AARON, a Moor, beloved by Tamora

A CAPTAIN

A MESSENGER

A CLOWN

TAMORA, Queen of the Goths

LAVINIA, daughter to Titus Andronicus

A NURSE, and a black CHILD

Romans and Goths, Senators, Tribunes, Officers, Soldiers, and Attendants

4

SCENE: Rome and the neighborhood

ACT 1

SCENE I. Rome. Before the Capitol

Flourish. Enter the TRIBUNES and SENATORS aloft; and then enter
below

SATURNINUS and his followers at one door, and BASSIANUS and his
followers at the other, with drums and trumpets

SATURNINUS.
Noble patricians, patrons of my right,
Defend the justice of my cause with arms;
And, countrymen, my loving followers,
Plead my successive title with your swords.

Noble patricians, supporters of my right to inherit,
defend the justice of my cause with weapons;
and, countrymen, my loving followers,
enforce my claim to inherit the title with your
swords.

I am his first born son that was the last
That ware the imperial diadem of Rome;
Then let my father's honours live in me,
Nor wrong mine age with this indignity.

I am the first born son of the man who last
wore the imperial crown of Rome;
so let my father's honours continue with me
and don't disrespect my status with such an insult.

BASSIANUS.
Romans, friends, followers, favourers of my right,
If ever Bassianus, Caesar's son,
Were gracious in the eyes of royal Rome,
Keep then this passage to the Capitol;
And suffer not dishonour to approach
The imperial seat, to virtue consecrate,
To justice, continence, and nobility;
But let desert in pure election shine;
And, Romans, fight for freedom in your choice.

Romans, friends, followers, supporters of my rights,
if Bassanius, son of Caesar,
was acceptable to the eyes of royal Rome,
then guard this passage to the Capitol;
don't allow a dishonourable man to approach
the emperor's throne, dedicated to virtue,
to justice, moderation and nobility;
choose the man who deserves the throne;
and, Romans, fight for your right to choose whom
you please.

Enter MARCUS ANDRONICUS aloft, with the crown

MARCUS.
Princes, that strive by factions and by friends

Princes, who fight with their parties and their
friends,

Ambitiously for rule and empery,

showing their ambition for power and the Emperor's
crown,

Know that the people of Rome, for whom we stand
A special party, have by common voice
In election for the Roman empery
Chosen Andronicus, surnamed Pius
For many good and great deserts to Rome.

I tell you that the people of Rome, of whom I am
special representative, have by unanimous choice
in the election for the Roman Emperor
chosen Andronicus, who has the surname Pius
due to his many good and great praiseworthy deeds
for Rome.

A nobler man, a braver warrior,
Lives not this day within the city walls.
He by the Senate is accited home,

There is not a nobler man nor a braver warrior
alive at this time inside the city walls.
He has been summoned home by the Senate

From weary wars against the barbarous Goths,	*from exhausting wars against the barbarous Goths.*
That with his sons, a terror to our foes,	*With his sons, a terror to our enemies,*
Hath yok'd a nation strong, train'd up in arms.	*he has conquered a strong nation who were well trained in warfare.*
Ten years are spent since first he undertook	*It is ten years since he first took up*
This cause of Rome, and chastised with arms	*the cause of Rome and punished our enemies' pride*
Our enemies' pride; five times he hath return'd	*with force; five times he has returned*
Bleeding to Rome, bearing his valiant sons	*wounded to Rome, carrying his brave sons*
In coffins from the field; and at this day	*in coffins from the field and today*
To the monument of that Andronici	*he has made a sacrifice of atonement*
Done sacrifice of expiation,	*at the Andronicus tomb,*
And slain the noblest prisoner of the Goths.	*and killed the noblest prisoner of the Goths.*
And now at last, laden with honour's spoils,	*And now at last, weighed down with the rewards of honour,*
Returns the good Andronicus to Rome,	*the good Andronicus has come back to Rome,*
Renowned Titus, flourishing in arms.	*the great Titus, at the peak of his powers.*
Let us entreat, by honour of his name	*We urge you, in honour of the name*
Whom worthily you would have now succeed,	*of the one whom you now wish to havea worthy inheritor,*
And in the Capitol and Senate's right,	*and out of respect for the rights of the Senate and the Capitol,*
Whom you pretend to honour and adore,	*which you claim to honour and worship,*
That you withdraw you and abate your strength,	*that you withdraw and disarm,*
Dismiss your followers, and, as suitors should,	*dismiss your followers and, as petitioners should,*
Plead your deserts in peace and humbleness.	*put your case peacefully and humbly.*

SATURNINUS.

How fair the Tribune speaks to calm my thoughts.	*The Tribune's fair speech calms my thoughts.*

BASSIANUS.

Marcus Andronicus, so I do affy	*Marcus Andronicus, I have so much faith*
In thy uprightness and integrity,	*in your honesty and integrity,*
And so I love and honour thee and thine,	*and so much love and honour for you and yours,*
Thy noble brother Titus and his sons,	*your noble brother Titus and his sons,*
And her to whom my thoughts are humbled all,	*and she whom I always worship,*
Gracious Lavinia, Rome's rich ornament,	*gracious Lavinia, Rome's rich decoration,*
That I will here dismiss my loving friends,	*that I will now dismiss my devoted followers*
And to my fortunes and the people's favour	*and let my case be judged on its merits*
Commit my cause in balance to be weigh'd.	*by my fortune and by the people.*
Exeunt the soldiers of BASSIANUS	

SATURNINUS.

Friends, that have been thus forward in my right,	*My friends who have been advocating my claim,*
I thank you all and here dismiss you all,	*I thank you all, and dismiss you,*
And to the love and favour of my country	*and I submit both myself and my cause*
Commit myself, my person, and the cause.	*to the love and kindness of my country.*
Exeunt the soldiers of SATURNINUS	
Rome, be as just and gracious unto me	*Rome, be as just and generous to me*

As I am confident and kind to thee.
Open the gates and let me in.

BASSIANUS.
Tribunes, and me, a poor competitor.
[Flourish. They go up into the Senate House]

Enter a CAPTAIN

CAPTAIN.
Romans, make way. The good Andronicus,
Patron of virtue, Rome's best champion,
Successful in the battles that he fights,
With honour and with fortune is return'd
From where he circumscribed with his sword
And brought to yoke the enemies of Rome.
Sound drums and trumpets, and then enter MARTIUS and MUTIUS, two of TITUS' sons; and then two
men bearing a coffin covered with black; then LUCIUS and QUINTUS, two other sons; then TITUS
ANDRONICUS; and then TAMORA the Queen of Goths, with her three sons, ALARBUS,
DEMETRIUS, and CHIRON, with AARON the Moor, and others, as many as can be. Then set down the
coffin and TITUS speaks

TITUS.
Hail, Rome, victorious in thy mourning weeds!

Lo, as the bark that hath discharg'd her fraught
Returns with precious lading to the bay
From whence at first she weigh'd her anchorage,
Cometh Andronicus, bound with laurel boughs,
To re-salute his country with his tears,
Tears of true joy for his return to Rome.
Thou great defender of this Capitol,
Stand gracious to the rites that we intend!
Romans, of five and twenty valiant sons,

Half of the number that King Priam had,
Behold the poor remains, alive and dead!
These that survive let Rome reward with love;
These that I bring unto their latest home,
With burial amongst their ancestors.
Here Goths have given me leave to sheathe my
sword.
Titus, unkind, and careless of thine own,
Why suffer'st thou thy sons, unburied yet,
To hover on the dreadful shore of Styx?

Make way to lay them by their brethren.
[They open the tomb]

as I am trusting and well disposed to you.
Open the gates and let me in.

And me, tribunes, a poor fellow candidate.

Romans, make way: the good Andronicus,
paragon of virtue, the greatest champion of Rome,
successful in the battles he fights,
has returned with honour and with fortune
from where he conquered the enemies of Rome
and confined them with his sword.

Greetings, Rome, victorious in your mourning
clothes!
See, like a ship which has unloaded its goods
and returns with a precious cargo to the bay
from which she first set out,
here comes Andronicus, wearing the laurel wreath,
to greet his country again with his tears,
genuine tears of joy at his return to Rome.
You great defender of this Capitol,
look favourably on the ceremonies we're planning.
Romans, you can see here the poor remains, alive
and dead
of twenty five brave sons,
half of the number that King Priam had:
let Rome reward the survivors with love;
these others I have brought to their last home,
to give them burial amongst their ancestors.
The Goths have allowed me to put away my
sword.
Titus, disrespectful and careless of your own family,
why have you allowed your sons to stay hovering
on the ghastly shores of the Styx due to you not
burying them?
Make way so I can lay them with their brothers.

8

There greet in silence, as the dead are wont,
And sleep in peace, slain in your country's wars.
O sacred receptacle of my joys,
Sweet cell of virtue and nobility,
How many sons hast thou of mine in store
That thou wilt never render to me more!

LUCIUS.
Give us the proudest prisoner of the Goths,
That we may hew his limbs, and on a pile
Ad manes fratrum sacrifice his flesh

Before this earthy prison of their bones,
That so the shadows be not unappeas'd,
Nor we disturb'd with prodigies on earth.

TITUS.
I give him you- the noblest that survives,
The eldest son of this distressed queen.

TAMORA.
Stay, Roman brethen! Gracious conqueror,
Victorious Titus, rue the tears I shed,
A mother's tears in passion for her son;
And if thy sons were ever dear to thee,
O, think my son to be as dear to me!
Sufficeth not that we are brought to Rome
To beautify thy triumphs, and return
Captive to thee and to thy Roman yoke;
But must my sons be slaughtered in the streets
For valiant doings in their country's cause?
O, if to fight for king and commonweal
Were piety in thine, it is in these.

Andronicus, stain not thy tomb with blood.
Wilt thou draw near the nature of the gods?
Draw near them then in being merciful.
Sweet mercy is nobility's true badge.
Thrice-noble Titus, spare my first-born son.

TITUS.
Patient yourself, madam, and pardon me.
These are their brethren whom your Goths beheld

Alive and dead; and for their brethren slain
Religiously they ask a sacrifice.
To this your son is mark'd, and die he must
T' appease their groaning shadows that are gone.

Greet them in silence, as the dead do,
and sleep in peace, killed in your country's wars.
O holy container of my happiness,
store room of virtue and nobility,
how many of my sons you have in there
that you will never return to me!

Give us the noblest prisoner of the Goths,
so we can hack his limbs off, and on a pyre
we can sacrifice his body to the ghosts of our brothers
in front of this earthly container of their bones,
so that the ghosts will not go unavenged,
and we won't have disturbing events on earth.

I give him to you; the noblest of the survivors,
the eldest son of this unhappy queen.

Stop, Roman brothers, gracious conqueror,
victorious Titus, pity the tears I am crying,
a mother's tears of grief for her son!
If you ever loved your sons
please believe that I love my son just as much.
Isn't it enough that we have been brought to Rome
to decorate your triumphant return,
enslaved to you and the orders of Rome?
Do my sons have to be slaughtered in the streets
for their brave efforts on behalf of their country?
Oh, if to fight for your King and country
is a good thing for you and yours, then it is for them as well.
Andronicus, don't stain your tomb with blood.
Do you want to become as godlike as possible?
Then try being as merciful as them.
Sweet mercy is the truest indicator of nobility:
thrice noble Titus, spare my oldest son.

Calm yourself, madam, and forgive me.
These are the brothers of those whom your Goths saw
alive and dead, and for their slain brothers
they are asking for a holy sacrifice.
Your son is marked out for this, and he must die
to satisfy the moaning ghosts of the dead.

LUCIUS.
Away with him, and make a fire straight;
And with our swords, upon a pile of wood,
Let's hew his limbs till they be clean consum'd.
Exeunt TITUS' SONS, with ALARBUS

Take him away, and make a fire at once;
and let's hack his limbs with our swords,
on the wooden pyre, until there is nothing left.

TAMORA.
O cruel, irreligious piety!

O cruel, blasphemous piety!

CHIRON.
Was never Scythia half so barbarous!

The Scythians were never half as barbarous!

DEMETRIUS.
Oppose not Scythia to ambitious Rome.
Alarbus goes to rest, and we survive
To tremble under Titus' threat'ning look.
Then, madam, stand resolv'd, but hope withal
The self-same gods that arm'd the Queen of Troy
With opportunity of sharp revenge
Upon the Thracian tyrant in his tent
May favour Tamora, the Queen of Goths-
When Goths were Goths and Tamora was queen-

To quit the bloody wrongs upon her foes.

Don't compare Scythia with the upstart Rome.
Alarbus goes to his rest and we survive
to tremble under the threatening look of Titus.
So, madam, resign yourself, but also hope
that the same gods that gave the Queen of Troy
the opportunity to take quick revenge upon
Polymestor in his tent
may also favour Tamora, the Queen of the Goths
(when the Goths were a people andTamora was
queen),
and help her revenge the bloody wrongs of her
enemies.

Re-enter LUCIUS, QUINTUS, MARTIUS, and
MUTIUS, the sons of ANDRONICUS, with their swords bloody

LUCIUS.
See, lord and father, how we have perform'd
Our Roman rites: Alarbus' limbs are lopp'd,

And entrails feed the sacrificing fire,
Whose smoke like incense doth perfume the sky.
Remaineth nought but to inter our brethren,
And with loud 'larums welcome them to Rome.

See, lord and father, how we have undertaken
our Roman ceremonies: Alarbus' limbs have been
chopped off
and his innards are feeding the sacrificial fire,
whose smoke perfumes the sky like incense.
There's nothing left to do but to bury our brothers
and with great trumpet calls welcome them to Rome.

TITUS.
Let it be so, and let Andronicus
Make this his latest farewell to their souls.
[Sound trumpets and lay the coffin in the tomb]
In peace and honour rest you here, my sons;
Rome's readiest champions, repose you here in rest,
Secure from worldly chances and mishaps!
Here lurks no treason, here no envy swells,
Here grow no damned drugs, here are no storms,
No noise, but silence and eternal sleep.

Let this happen, and let Andronicus
say his last goodbye to their souls.

Rest here in peace and honour, my sons;
Rome's greatest champions, lie here and rest,
safe from fickle fate and accidents.
There is no treason here, no envy,
there are no poisonous plants, there are no storms,
no noise, just silence and eternal sleep:

In peace and honour rest you here, my sons!

rest here in peace and honour, my sons.

Enter LAVINIA
LAVINIA.
In peace and honour live Lord Titus long;

May Lord Titus have a long life in peace and honour;

My noble lord and father, live in fame!
Lo, at this tomb my tributary tears
I render for my brethren's obsequies;
And at thy feet I kneel, with tears of joy
Shed on this earth for thy return to Rome.
O, bless me here with thy victorious hand,
Whose fortunes Rome's best citizens applaud!

my noble Lord and father, live through your fame!
See, at this tomb I add my own tears
to the funeral rites for my brothers,
and I kneel at your feet with tears of joy
falling on the earth for your return to Rome.
O bless me with your victorious hand,
whose actions are applauded by the greatest citizens
of Rome.

TITUS.
Kind Rome, that hast thus lovingly reserv'd
The cordial of mine age to glad my heart!

Sweet Rome, you have lovingly kept for me
the nourishment of my old age which gladdens my
heart.

Lavinia, live; outlive thy father's days,
And fame's eternal date, for virtue's praise!

Lavinia live, live longer than your father,
live longer than history, because of your great
virtue.

Enter, above, MARCUS ANDRONICUS and TRIBUNES;
re-enter SATURNINUS, BASSIANUS, and attendants

MARCUS.
Long live Lord Titus, my beloved brother,
Gracious triumpher in the eyes of Rome!

Long live Lord Titus, my beloved brother,
the great victor that all Rome can see!

TITUS.
Thanks, gentle Tribune, noble brother Marcus.

Thanks, kind Tribune, noble brother Marcus.

MARCUS.
And welcome, nephews, from successful wars,
You that survive and you that sleep in fame.
Fair lords, your fortunes are alike in all
That in your country's service drew your swords;
But safer triumph is this funeral pomp
That hath aspir'd to Solon's happiness
And triumphs over chance in honour's bed.

And welcome, nephews, back from successful wars,
you survivors and you glorious dead.
Fair lords, you have all followed the same path
in fighting for your country;
but those who have died are more secure
and have found the happiness Solon spoke of,
which is better than the short lived benefits of
honour.

Titus Andronicus, the people of Rome,
Whose friend in justice thou hast ever been,
Send thee by me, their Tribune and their trust,

Titus Andronicus, the people of Rome,
to whom you have always been a fair friend,
have sent you, via me, their Tribune and
representative,

This par]iament of white and spotless hue;
And name thee in election for the empire

this pure white candidate's gown,
and ask you to be a candidate for the Emperorship,

With these our late-deceased Emperor's sons:	alongside these sons of our recently departed Emperor.
Be candidatus then, and put it on,	So become a candidate and put it on,
And help to set a head on headless Rome.	and help to give direction to leaderless Rome.

TITUS.

A better head her glorious body fits	Her glorious body deserves a better head
Than his that shakes for age and feebleness.	than this one which is shaking with age and weakness.
What should I don this robe and trouble you?	Why should I put on this robe and cause you trouble?
Be chosen with proclamations to-day,	I could be elected and declared Emperor today,
To-morrow yield up rule, resign my life,	tomorrow I could die, give up my post,
And set abroad new business for you all?	and you'd have to do the whole business over again.
Rome, I have been thy soldier forty years,	Rome, I have been a soldier for you for forty years,
And led my country's strength successfully,	and led my country's armies successfully,
And buried one and twenty valiant sons,	I have buried twenty-one brave sons,
Knighted in field, slain manfully in arms,	who were knighted in battle, killed bravely in warfare
In right and service of their noble country.	in the justified service of their noble country:
Give me a staff of honour for mine age,	give me a staff of honour to support me in my old age,
But not a sceptre to control the world.	but not a sceptre to control the whole world.
Upright he held it, lords, that held it last.	The last one who had it, lords, held it in a firm grip.

MARCUS.

Titus, thou shalt obtain and ask the empery.	Titus, you shall have the emperorship if you ask for it.

SATURNINUS.

Proud and ambitious Tribune, canst thou tell?	Arrogant and ambitious Tribune, how do you know this?

TITUS.

Patience, Prince Saturninus.	Calm down, Prince Saturninus.

SATURNINUS.

Romans, do me right.	Romans, support my rights.
Patricians, draw your swords, and sheathe them not	Patricians, draw your swords, and do not sheathe them
Till Saturninus be Rome's Emperor.	until Saturninus is emperor of Rome.
Andronicus, would thou were shipp'd to hell	Andronicus, I'll see you in hell
Rather than rob me of the people's hearts!	before you steal the people's hearts from me!

LUCIUS.

Proud Saturnine, interrupter of the good	Arrogant Saturnine, you have interrupted noble minded
That noble-minded Titus means to thee!	Titus when he was announcing good things for you!

TITUS.
Content thee, Prince; I will restore to thee

Be at peace, Prince; I will give the people's hearts back to you,

The people's hearts, and wean them from themselves. *and reconcile them to not getting what they want.*

BASSIANUS.
Andronicus, I do not flatter thee,
But honour thee, and will do till I die.
My faction if thou strengthen with thy friends,
I will most thankful be; and thanks to men
Of noble minds is honourable meed.

Andronicus, I won't flatter you,
but I do honour you, and I will do until I die.
If you strengthen my party with your friends,
I will be most grateful; and to men of noble
minds thanks is an honourable reward.

TITUS.
People of Rome, and people's Tribunes here,
I ask your voices and your suffrages:
Will ye bestow them friendly on Andronicus?

People of Rome, and the people's Tribunes here,
I ask you to cast your votes:
will you give them on good terms to Andronicus?

TRIBUNES.
To gratify the good Andronicus,
And gratulate his safe return to Rome,
The people will accept whom he admits.

To please the good Andronicus,
and to celebrate his safe return to Rome,
the people will accept whoever he chooses.

TITUS.
Tribunes, I thank you; and this suit I make,
That you create our Emperor's eldest son,
Lord Saturnine; whose virtues will, I hope,
Reflect on Rome as Titan's rays on earth,
And ripen justice in this commonweal.
Then, if you will elect by my advice,
Crown him, and say 'Long live our Emperor!'

Tribunes, I thank you; and I ask you this,
that you choose our Emperor's oldest son,
Lord Saturnine; I hope his virtues will
light up Rome as the sun does the earth,
and help justice to grow in this kingdom—
so if you will be guided by my advice,
crown him and say, 'Long live our Emperor!'

MARCUS.
With voices and applause of every sort,
Patricians and plebeians, we create
Lord Saturninus Rome's great Emperor;
And say 'Long live our Emperor Saturnine!'
[A long flourish till they come down]

With your voices and every sort of applause,
patricians and people, we create
Lord Saturninus the great emperor of Rome;
and say 'Long live our Emperor Saturnine!'

SATURNINUS.
Titus Andronicus, for thy favours done
To us in our election this day
I give thee thanks in part of thy deserts,

And will with deeds requite thy gentleness;
And for an onset, Titus, to advance
Thy name and honourable family,
Lavinia will I make my emperess,

Titus Andronicus, for the favours you have done
for me in helping my election today
I give you my thanks as part payment of your reward,
and will repay the rest of your kindness with deeds;
and for a beginning, Titus, to promote
your name and that of your honourable family,
I will make Lavinia my Empress,

Rome's royal mistress, mistress of my heart,
And in the sacred Pantheon her espouse.
Tell me, Andronicus, doth this motion please thee?

TITUS.
It doth, my worthy lord, and in this match
I hold me highly honoured of your Grace,
And here in sight of Rome, to Saturnine,

King and commander of our commonweal,
The wide world's Emperor, do I consecrate
My sword, my chariot, and my prisoners,
Presents well worthy Rome's imperious lord;
Receive them then, the tribute that I owe,
Mine honour's ensigns humbled at thy feet.

SATURNINUS.
Thanks, noble Titus, father of my life.
How proud I am of thee and of thy gifts
Rome shall record; and when I do forget
The least of these unspeakable deserts,
Romans, forget your fealty to me.

TITUS. [To TAMORA]
Now, madam, are you prisoner to an emperor;
To him that for your honour and your state
Will use you nobly and your followers.

SATURNINUS.
[Aside] A goodly lady, trust me; of the hue
That I would choose, were I to choose anew.-
Clear up, fair Queen, that cloudy countenance;
Though chance of war hath wrought this change of cheer,
Thou com'st not to be made a scorn in Rome-
Princely shall be thy usage every way.
Rest on my word, and let not discontent
Daunt all your hopes. Madam, he comforts you

Can make you greater than the Queen of Goths.

Lavinia, you are not displeas'd with this?

LAVINIA.
Not I, my lord, sith true nobility
Warrants these words in princely courtesy.

the Royal mistress of Rome, mistress of my heart,
and I will marry her in the holy Pantheon.
Tell me, Andronicus, does this idea please you?

It does, my noble Lord, and I take this marriage
as a great honour from your Grace,
and here with all Rome as witnesses, I give Saturnine,
king and commander of our nation,
the Emperor of the wide world,
my sword, my chariot and my prisoners,
presents whichRome's Imperial Lord well deserves;
so take them, the tribute that I owe you,
the symbols of my honour laid down at your feet.

Thanks, noble Titus, father of my life.
Rome shall take note of how pleased I am with you
and your gifts; and when I forget
the smallest of these indescribable rewards,
Romans, you can renounce your loyalty to me.

Now, madam, you are an emperor's prisoner;

because of your honour and your high rank
he will treat you and your followers with respect.

A fine lady, my goodness; of the colour
that I would choose, if I were to choose another–
fair Queen, take off that frown;
although the fortunes of war have made you miserable,
you will not be badly treated in Rome–
you shall be treated as royalty in every way.
Take my word for it, and don't let unhappiness
take over your whole life. Madam, the one who is comforting you
can give you a greater position than Queen of the Goths.
Lavinia, this doesn't upset you?

Not me, my lord, since yourtrue nobility
guarantees that these words are just the courtesy a
should show.

SATURNINUS.
Thanks, sweet Lavinia. Romans, let us go.
Ransomless here we set our prisoners free.
Proclaim our honours, lords, with trump and drum.

Thanks, sweet Lavinia. Romans, let us go.
We set these prisoners free without a ransom.
Announce my new position, lords, with trumpets and
drums.

[Flourish]

BASSIANUS.
Lord Titus, by your leave, this maid is mine.
[Seizing LAVINIA]

Lord Titus, if you'll excuse me, this girl is mine.

TITUS.
How, sir! Are you in earnest then, my lord?

What, sir! Are you serious then, my lord?

BASSIANUS.
Ay, noble Titus, and resolv'd withal
To do myself this reason and this right.

Yes, noble Titus, and I am determined
to claim my reasonable rights.

MARCUS.
Suum cuique is our Roman justice:
This prince in justice seizeth but his own.

Each is entitled to his own is our Roman law:
the Prince is only taking what is his own by law.

LUCIUS.
And that he will and shall, if Lucius live.

And he will have it, as long as Lucius is alive.

TITUS.
Traitors, avaunt! Where is the Emperor's guard?
Treason, my lord- Lavinia is surpris'd!

Traitors, be gone! Where are the emperor's guards?
There is treason, my lord–Lavinia has been
ambushed!

SATURNINUS.
Surpris'd! By whom?

Ambushed! By whom?

BASSIANUS.
By him that justly may
Bear his betroth'd from all the world away.
Exeunt BASSIANUS and MARCUS with LAVINIA

By the one who has every right
to carry his fiancée away from all others.

MUTIUS.
Brothers, help to convey her hence away,
And with my sword I'll keep this door safe.
 Exeunt LUCIUS, QUINTUS, and MARTIUS

Brothers, help to get her away from here,
and I'll block this door with my sword.

TITUS.
Follow, my lord, and I'll soon bring her back.

Let's follow her, my lord, and I'll soon bring her
back.

MUTIUS.

My lord, you pass not here.

My lord, you cannot go through here.

TITUS.
What, villain boy!
Bar'st me my way in Rome?

What, you villainous boy!
Do you block my way in Rome?

MUTIUS.
Help, Lucius, help!

Help, Lucius, help!

TITUS kills him. During the fray, exeunt SATURNINUS,
TAMORA, DEMETRIUS, CHIRON, and AARON
Re-enter Lucius

LUCIUS.
My lord, you are unjust, and more than so:
In wrongful quarrel you have slain your son.

My Lord, you are unjust, and more than unjust:
in an unjust quarrel you have killed your son.

TITUS.
Nor thou nor he are any sons of mine;
My sons would never so dishonour me.
 Re-enter aloft the EMPEROR
with TAMORA and her two Sons, and AARON the Moor
Traitor, restore Lavinia to the Emperor.

Neither you nor he are any sons of mine;
my real sons would never shame me like this.

Traitor, give Lavinia back to the Emperor.

LUCIUS.
Dead, if you will; but not to be his wife,
That is another's lawful promis'd love. Exit

Dead, if you like; but not as his wife,
when she is lawfully engaged to someone else.

SATURNINUS.
No, Titus, no; the Emperor needs her not,
Nor her, nor thee, nor any of thy stock.
I'll trust by leisure him that mocks me once;
Thee never, nor thy traitorous haughty sons,

Confederates all thus to dishonour me.
Was there none else in Rome to make a stale

But Saturnine? Full well, Andronicus,
Agree these deeds with that proud brag of thine
That saidst I begg'd the empire at thy hands.

No, Titus, no; the Emperor doesn't need her,
not her, nor you, nor any of your family.
I can hardly trust someone who makes a fool of me;
I shall never trust you, or your traitorous arrogant
sons,
who have all joined together to dishonour me.
Was there nobody else in Rome to use as the butt of
your jokes
but Saturnine? This sort of behaviour, Andronicus,
completely matches that proud boast of yours
that claims that I begged for the Empire from you.

TITUS.
O monstrous! What reproachful words are these?

This is monstrous! What is this criticism?

SATURNINUS.
But go thy ways; go, give that changing piece

To him that flourish'd for her with his sword.
A valiant son-in-law thou shalt enjoy;

Just go about your business; go on, give that fickle
woman
to the one who waved his sword about for her.
You shall have a brave son-in-law;

One fit to bandy with thy lawless sons,
To ruffle in the commonwealth of Rome.

one suited to brawling with your lawless sons,
to stir up the peace of the Kingdom of Rome.

TITUS.
These words are razors to my wounded heart.

These words cut my wounded heart like razors.

SATURNINUS.
And therefore, lovely Tamora, Queen of Goths,
That, like the stately Phoebe 'mongst her nymphs,
Dost overshine the gallant'st dames of Rome,
If thou be pleas'd with this my sudden choice,
Behold, I choose thee, Tamora, for my bride
And will create thee Emperess of Rome.
Speak, Queen of Goths, dost thou applaud my choice?
And here I swear by all the Roman gods-
Sith priest and holy water are so near,
And tapers burn so bright, and everything
In readiness for Hymenaeus stand-
I will not re-salute the streets of Rome,
Or climb my palace, till from forth this place
I lead espous'd my bride along with me.

And so, lovely Tamora, Queen of Goths,
who, like the glorious Diana amongst her nymphs,
outshines the finest looking women in Rome,
if you will agree to my sudden choice,
I tell you I choose you, Tamora, as my bride
and will make you Empress of Rome.
Speak, Queen of Goths, do you applaud my choice?
And I swear by all the Roman gods–
since priests and holy water are so near,
and the candles burn so bright, and everything
is ready for a wedding–
I will not go back out into the streets of Rome,
or go up to my palace, until I leave this place
leading my bride along with me.

TAMORA.
And here in sight of heaven to Rome I swear,
If Saturnine advance the Queen of Goths,
She will a handmaid be to his desires,
A loving nurse, a mother to his youth.

And here in the sight of heaven I swear to Rome,
that if Saturnine advances the Queen of the Goths,
she will assist him in everything he desires,
be a loving nurse and a mother to his youth.

SATURNINUS.
Ascend, fair Queen, Pantheon. Lords, accompany

Your noble Emperor and his lovely bride,
Sent by the heavens for Prince Saturnine,
Whose wisdom hath her fortune conquered;
There shall we consummate our spousal rites.
Exeunt all but TITUS

Come up, my fair Queen, to the Pantheon. Lords, accompany
your noble emperor and his lovely bride,
sent from heaven for Prince Saturnine,
who has wisely overcome her misfortune;
in the Pantheon we shall settle our marriage.

TITUS.
I am not bid to wait upon this bride.
Titus, when wert thou wont to walk alone,
Dishonoured thus, and challenged of wrongs?
Re-enter MARCUS,
and TITUS' SONS, LUCIUS, QUINTUS, and MARTIUS

I'm not invited to this wedding.
Titus, since when have you had to walk alone,
disgraced like this, and accused of crimes?

MARCUS.
O Titus, see, O, see what thou hast done!
In a bad quarrel slain a virtuous son.

Oh Titus, see, oh see what you have done!
In an unjustified quarrel you have killed a good son.

TITUS.
No, foolish Tribune, no; no son of mine-
Nor thou, nor these, confederates in the deed
That hath dishonoured all our family;
Unworthy brother and unworthy sons!

LUCIUS.
But let us give him burial, as becomes;
Give Mutius burial with our bretheren.

TITUS.
Traitors, away! He rests not in this tomb.
This monument five hundred years hath stood,
Which I have sumptuously re-edified;
Here none but soldiers and Rome's servitors
Repose in fame; none basely slain in brawls.
Bury him where you can, he comes not here.

MARCUS.
My lord, this is impiety in you.
My nephew Mutius' deeds do plead for him;
He must be buried with his bretheren.

QUINTUS & MARTIUS.
And shall, or him we will accompany.

TITUS.
'And shall!' What villain was it spake that word?

QUINTUS.
He that would vouch it in any place but here.

TITUS.
What, would you bury him in my despite?

MARCUS.
No, noble Titus, but entreat of thee
To pardon Mutius and to bury him.

TITUS.
Marcus, even thou hast struck upon my crest,
And with these boys mine honour thou hast
wounded.
My foes I do repute you every one;
So trouble me no more, but get you gone.

MARTIUS.

No, foolish Tribune, no; no son of mine—
nor are you, nor are these, partners in the deed
that has brought dishonour on all our family;
unworthy brother and unworthy sons!

But let us give him a fitting burial;
bury Mutius with our brothers.

Go away, traitors! He shall not rest in this tomb.
This monument has stood for five hundred years,
and I have rebuilt it richly;
nobody but soldiers and servants of Rome
rest here in honour; not people killed in low brawls.
Bury him where you like, he's not coming in here.

My lord, this is not pious.
My nephew Mutius' accomplishments speak for him;
he must be buried with his brothers.

And he shall, or we will follow him.

'And shall!' What villain was it who said that?

One who would fight for it anywhere but here.

What, you would bury him against my wishes?

No, noble Titus, but we beg you
to pardon Mutius and to bury him.

Marcus, you have struck me on the helmet,
and with these boys you have assaulted my
honour.
I count you all as my enemies,
so stop bothering me and go away.

He is not with himself; let us withdraw.

He's not himself; let's go away.

QUINTUS.
Not I, till Mutius' bones be buried.
[The BROTHER and the SONS kneel]

I will not, until Mutius has been buried.

MARCUS.
Brother, for in that name doth nature plead-

Brother, for that is the name which should make you-

QUINTUS.
Father, and in that name doth nature speak-

Father, for that is the name which should make you-

TITUS.
Speak thou no more, if all the rest will speed.

Say no more, if the rest is like this.

MARCUS.
Renowned Titus, more than half my soul-

Renowned Titus, who can claim more than half my soul-

LUCIUS.
Dear father, soul and substance of us all-

Dear father, the soul and body of us all-

MARCUS.
Suffer thy brother Marcus to inter
His noble nephew here in virtue's nest,
That died in honour and Lavinia's cause.
Thou art a Roman- be not barbarous.
The Greeks upon advice did bury Ajax,
That slew himself; and wise Laertes' son
Did graciously plead for his funerals.
Let not young Mutius, then, that was thy joy,

Be barr'd his entrance here.

Allow your brother Marcus to place
his noble nephew here in the home of virtue,
who died honourably fighting for Lavinia.
You are a Roman - don't act like a barbarian.
After thinking about it the Greeks buried Ajax,
who had killed himself; and wise Ulysses
graciously argued for a proper funeral.
So don't let young Mutius, who was the apple of your eye,
be blocked from a burial here.

TITUS.
Rise, Marcus, rise;
The dismal'st day is this that e'er I saw,
To be dishonoured by my sons in Rome!
Well, bury him, and bury me the next.
[They put MUTIUS in the tomb]

Get up, Marcus;
this is the worst day of my life,
being dishonoured by my sons in Rome!
Well, bury him, and bury me afterwards.

LUCIUS.
There lie thy bones, sweet Mutius, with thy friends,

Till we with trophies do adorn thy tomb.

Let your bones lie there, sweet Mutius, with your friends,
until we decorate your tomb with trophies.

ALL.
[Kneeling] No man shed tears for noble Mutius;
He lives in fame that died in virtue's cause.

No man should weep for noble Mutius,
he lives on in his fame for dying in the cause of

MARCUS.
My lord- to step out of these dreary dumps-
How comes it that the subtle Queen of Goths
Is of a sudden thus advanc'd in Rome?

TITUS.
I know not, Marcus, but I know it is-
Whether by device or no, the heavens can tell.
Is she not, then, beholding to the man
That brought her for this high good turn so far?

MARCUS.
Yes, and will nobly him remunerate.
Flourish. Re-enter the EMPEROR, TAMORA
and her two SONS, with the MOOR, at one door;
at the other door, BASSIANUS and LAVINIA, with others

SATURNINUS.
So, Bassianus, you have play'd your prize:
God give you joy, sir, of your gallant bride!

BASSIANUS.
And you of yours, my lord! I say no more,
Nor wish no less; and so I take my leave.

SATURNINUS.
Traitor, if Rome have law or we have power,
Thou and thy faction shall repent this rape.

BASSIANUS.
Rape, call you it, my lord, to seize my own,
My true betrothed love, and now my wife?
But let the laws of Rome determine all;
Meanwhile am I possess'd of that is mine.

SATURNINUS.
'Tis good, sir. You are very short with us;
But if we live we'll be as sharp with you.

BASSIANUS.
My lord, what I have done, as best I may,
Answer I must, and shall do with my life.
Only thus much I give your Grace to know:
By all the duties that I owe to Rome,
This noble gentleman, Lord Titus here,
Is in opinion and in honour wrong'd,
That, in the rescue of Lavinia,

virtue.

My lord - to move on from this sad mood -
why has the cunning Queen of the Goths
suddenly become promoted so high in Rome?

I don't know, Marcus, but I know it's happened -
whether it's a plot or not, only heaven knows.
Does she owe nothing, then, to the man
who brought her so far for such honours?

Yes, and she will pay him generously.

So, Bassanius, you have won your bout:
may heaven give you pleasure in your noble bride!

And the same to you, my lord!I'll say no more,
and I don't wish for any less; and so I'll say
goodbye.

You traitor, if Rome has laws or I have power
you and your party will regret this rape.

Do you call it rape, my lord, to claim what's mine,
my true fiancee, and now my wife?
But let the law of Rome decide the matter;
for now I have what's mine.

Very well, sir.You are very snappy with us;
but as long as I live you might find I can snap at
you.

My lord, I will defend what I have done as
well as I can, and I'm prepared to pay with my life.
But I want to say this to your grace:
by all the service I owe to Rome,
this noble gentleman here, Lord Titus,
has been wrongly accused of disloyalty,
for he killed his youngest son himself

20

With his own hand did slay his youngest son, *when trying to recapture Lavinia,*
In zeal to you, and highly mov'd to wrath *out of loyalty to you and because he was angry*
To be controll'd in that he frankly gave. *to be thwarted in what he freely gave you.*
Receive him then to favour, Saturnine, *So give him your goodwill, Saturnine,*
That hath express'd himself in all his deeds *someone who has shown him in all his actions*
A father and a friend to thee and Rome. *to be a father and a friend to you and to Rome.*

TITUS.
Prince Bassianus, leave to plead my deeds. *Prince Bassanius, let me speak for myself.*
'Tis thou and those that have dishonoured me. *It's you and these others who have dishonoured me.*
Rome and the righteous heavens be my judge *Rome and the honest heavens can judge*
How I have lov'd and honoured Saturnine! *how I have loved and honoured Saturnine!*

TAMORA.
My worthy lord, if ever Tamora *My worthy lord, if Tamora ever*
Were gracious in those princely eyes of thine, *found any favour in your princely eyes,*
Then hear me speak indifferently for all; *then let me speak impartially,*
And at my suit, sweet, pardon what is past. *and do as I ask, my sweet, and forgive the past.*

SATURNINUS.
What, madam! be dishonoured openly, *What, madam! Be openly disrespected,*
And basely put it up without revenge? *and meekly put up with it without revenge?*

TAMORA.
Not so, my lord; the gods of Rome forfend *No, my lord. May the cause of Rome never allow*
I should be author to dishonour you! *need to show disrespect for you.*
But on mine honour dare I undertake *But I'm prepared to swear*
For good Lord Titus' innocence in all, *for good Lord Titus' innocence in everything,*
Whose fury not dissembled speaks his griefs. *whose genuine anger speaks of his sorrow.*
Then at my suit look graciously on him; *So at my request look kindly on him;*
Lose not so noble a friend on vain suppose, *don't lose such a noble friend through imagined wrongs,*

Nor with sour looks afflict his gentle heart. *nor hurt his gentle heart with dirty looks.*
[Aside to SATURNINUS] My lord, be rul'd by me, *[Aside to Saturninus]*
be won at last; *My Lord, take my advice, be won over,*
Dissemble all your griefs and discontents. *hide all your sorrow and anger.*
You are but newly planted in your throne; *You have only just gained your throne;*
Lest, then, the people, and patricians too, *in case the people, and the patricians too,*
Upon a just survey take Titus' part, *when they think about it take Titus' side,*
And so supplant you for ingratitude, *and so overthrow you for ingratitude,*
Which Rome reputes to be a heinous sin, *which Rome regards as a terrible sin,*
Yield at entreats, and then let me alone: *give in to my requests–and then leave it to me:*
I'll find a day to massacre them all, *I'll choose a time to massacre them all,*
And raze their faction and their family, *and destroy their party and their family,*
The cruel father and his traitorous sons, *the cruel father and his traitorous sons*
To whom I sued for my dear son's life; *whom I begged for my dear son's life,*
And make them know what 'tis to let a queen *and I shall let them know the thing they've done*
Kneel in the streets and beg for grace in vain.- *in making a Queen kneel in the streets and beg for*

21

Come, come, sweet Emperor; come, Andronicus.
Take up this good old man, and cheer the heart
That dies in tempest of thy angry frown.

SATURNINUS.
Rise, Titus, rise; my Empress hath prevail'd.

TITUS.
I thank your Majesty and her, my lord;
These words, these looks, infuse new life in me.

TAMORA.
Titus, I am incorporate in Rome,
A Roman now adopted happily,
And must advise the Emperor for his good.
This day all quarrels die, Andronicus;
And let it be mine honour, good my lord,
That I have reconcil'd your friends and you.
For you, Prince Bassianus, I have pass'd
My word and promise to the Emperor
That you will be more mild and tractable.
And fear not, lords- and you, Lavinia.
By my advice, all humbled on your knees,
You shall ask pardon of his Majesty.

LUCIUS.
We do, and vow to heaven and to his Highness
That what we did was mildly as we might,
Tend'ring our sister's honour and our own.

MARCUS.
That on mine honour here do I protest.

SATURNINUS.
Away, and talk not; trouble us no more.

TAMORA.
Nay, nay, sweet Emperor, we must all be friends.
The Tribune and his nephews kneel for grace.
I will not be denied. Sweet heart, look back.

SATURNINUS.
Marcus, for thy sake, and thy brother's here,

And at my lovely Tamora's entreats,
I do remit these young men's heinous faults.

kindness in vain.
[Aloud]
Come, come, sweet Emperor—come, Andronicus—
tell this good old man to get up, and cheer the heart
that is dying in the storm of your angry frown.

Get up, Titus, get up; my Empress has won.

My Lord, I thank both you and her;
these words and these looks give me new life.

Titus, I have become part of Rome,
now a happily naturalised Roman,
and I must advise the Emperor for the best.
All quarrels died today, Andronicus;
and let it be my privilege, good my lord,
to have reconciled your friends and you.
For you, Prince Bassanius, I have given
my word and promise to the Emperor
that you will be milder and more obedient.
And do not worry, Lords—nor you, Lavinia:
I advise you all to go down on your knees
and ask for his Majesty's pardon.

We do, and we vow to heaven and to his Highness
that we only did the least that we could do
to protect the honour of our sister and ourselves.

I swear to that on my honour.

Go away, and don't talk; don't bother us any more.

No, no, sweet Emperor, we must all be friends.
The Tribune and his nephews kneel for forgiveness.
I won't be denied. Sweetheart, turn around.

Marcus, for your sake, and for the sake of your
brother here,
and at the pleading of my lovely Tamora,
I forgive these young men's serious crimes.

They stand up.

Lavinia, though you left me like a churl,
I found a friend; and sure as death I swore
I would not part a bachelor from the priest.
Come, if the Emperor's court can feast two brides,

You are my guest, Lavinia, and your friends.
This day shall be a love-day, Tamora.

TITUS.
To-morrow, and it please your Majesty
To hunt the panther and the hart with me,
With horn and hound we'll give your Grace bonjour.

SATURNINUS.
Be it so, Titus, and gramercy too.
Exeunt. Sound trumpets

Lavinia, though you parted from me unkindly,
I found someone else; and as sure as death I swore
I would not walk away from the priest as a bachelor.
Come, if the Emperor's court can hold two wedding
breakfasts,
you are my guest, Lavinia, and your friends.
Today shall be a day of love, Tamora.

Tomorrow, if your Majesty pleases, I should
like to invite you to hunt panthers and deer with me,
and we'll welcome your Grace with the horn and the
dogs.

Let's do that Titus, and I thank you for it.

ACT II

SCENE I. Rome. Before the palace

Enter AARON

AARON.
Now climbeth Tamora Olympus' top,
Safe out of Fortune's shot, and sits aloft,
Secure of thunder's crack or lightning flash,
Advanc'd above pale envy's threat'ning reach.
As when the golden sun salutes the morn,
And, having gilt the ocean with his beams,
Gallops the zodiac in his glistening coach
And overlooks the highest-peering hills,
So Tamora.
Upon her wit doth earthly honour wait,
And virtue stoops and trembles at her frown.

Then, Aaron, arm thy heart and fit thy thoughts
To mount aloft with thy imperial mistress,
And mount her pitch whom thou in triumph long.
Hast prisoner held, fett'red in amorous chains,
And faster bound to Aaron's charming eyes
Than is Prometheus tied to Caucasus.
Away with slavish weeds and servile thoughts!
I will be bright and shine in pearl and gold,
To wait upon this new-made emperess.
To wait, said I? To wanton with this queen,
This goddess, this Semiramis, this nymph,
This siren that will charm Rome's Saturnine,
And see his shipwreck and his commonweal's.
Hullo! what storm is this?
Enter CHIRON and DEMETRIUS, braving

DEMETRIUS.
Chiron, thy years wants wit, thy wits wants edge

And manners, to intrude where I am grac'd,

And may, for aught thou knowest, affected be.

CHIRON.
Demetrius, thou dost over-ween in all;
And so in this, to bear me down with braves.
'Tis not the difference of a year or two
Makes me less gracious or thee more fortunate:

I am as able and as fit as thou

Now Tamora has reached the summit of Olympus,
she can't be harmed by fortune, and sits on high,
safe from the thunder and lightning,
promoted beyond the reach of envious people.
It's like when the golden sun comes in the morning
and, having gilded the ocean with his beams,
he gallops across the sky in his shining coach
and looks down on the highest mountains,
that's Tamora.
Honourable men wait for her decisions,
and goodness bows down and trembles when she frowns.
So, Aaron, strengthen your heart and mind
to climb up to your imperial mistress,
join her at the top, the one whom you have
kept prisoner for so long, bound by chains of love,
tied more securely to Aaron's enchanting eyes
than Prometheus is tied to his rock.
No more slave's clothing and servant's thoughts!
I will be bright, and shine with pearls and gold
when I serve this newly made Empress.
Serve, did I say?—To frolic with this Queen,
this goddess, this Semiramis, this nymph,
this siren that will charm Rome's Saturnine
and cause him and his kingdom to be wrecked.
Hello, what's this storm?

Chiron, you need wit to match your age, and your wits
lacking in sharpness and manners, as you are
intruding where I am welcomed
and for all you know am loved.

Demetrius, you are always so arrogant;
this is no exception, trying to shout me down.
There's only a difference of a year or two
which doesn't make me less gracious or you more blessed:
I'm just as able and as suitable as you

To serve and to deserve my mistress' grace;
And that my sword upon thee shall approve,
And plead my passions for Lavinia's love.

to serve my mistress and deserve her kindness;
and I shall prove that to you with my sword,
and show how much I want Lavinia's love.

AARON.
[Aside] Clubs, clubs! These lovers will not keep the peace.

Call the watchmen! These lovers will not keep the peace.

DEMETRIUS.
Why, boy, although our mother, unadvis'd,
Gave you a dancing rapier by your side,
Are you so desperate grown to threat your friends?
Go to; have your lath glued within your sheath

Till you know better how to handle it.

Why, boy, although our mother, unwisely,
gave you an ornamental sword to wear,
have you become so keen to threaten your friends?
Give over; have your toy sword glued inside its sheath
until you have a better idea of how to handle it.

CHIRON.
Meanwhile, sir, with the little skill I have,
Full well shalt thou perceive how much I dare.

In the meantime, sir, with what little skill I have,
you will see how eager I am to use it.

DEMETRIUS.
Ay, boy, grow ye so brave? [They draw]

Oh yes, boy, you're that brave are you?

AARON.
[Coming forward] Why, how now, lords!
So near the Emperor's palace dare ye draw

And maintain such a quarrel openly?
Full well I wot the ground of all this grudge:
I would not for a million of gold
The cause were known to them it most concerns;

Nor would your noble mother for much more
Be so dishonoured in the court of Rome.
For shame, put up.

Why, what's all this, lords!
Do you dare to draw weapons so close to the Emperor's palace
and fight each other so openly?
I'm well aware of why you're fighting:
I wouldn't take a million pounds
to let the ones who are most closely involved know about it;
and your noble mother would turn down even more
rather than be so dishonoured in the court of Rome.
For shame, put away your weapons.

DEMETRIUS.
Not I, till I have sheath'd
My rapier in his bosom, and withal
Thrust those reproachful speeches down his throat
That he hath breath'd in my dishonour here.

I won't, until I have put away
my rapier in his heart, and what's more
shoved the reproaches with which he has
dishonoured me back down his throat.

CHIRON.
For that I am prepar'd and full resolv'd,
Foul-spoken coward, that thund'rest with thy tongue,

And with thy weapon nothing dar'st perform.

I'm ready for that and well up to it,
you dirty mouthed coward, you roar with your tongue,
and don't dare do anything with your weapon.

AARON.
Away, I say!
Now, by the gods that warlike Goths adore,
This petty brabble will undo us all.
Why, lords, and think you not how dangerous

It is to jet upon a prince's right?
What, is Lavinia then become so loose,
Or Bassianus so degenerate,
That for her love such quarrels may be broach'd
Without controlment, justice, or revenge?
Young lords, beware; an should the Empress know
This discord's ground, the music would not please.

That's enough, I say!
Now, by the gods of the warlike Goths,
this petty quarrel will get us all in trouble.
Why, lords, haven't you thought about how
dangerous
it is to encroach on the rights of princes?
What, has Lavinia become such a tart,
or Bassianus become so degenerate,
that you can start a fight for her love
without restraint, justice, or punishment?
Beware, young lords–and if the Empress found out
what started this argument, things would not go
well.

CHIRON.
I care not, I, knew she and all the world:

I love Lavinia more than all the world.

I don't care, I wouldn't care if she and all the world
knew:
I love Lavinia more than all the world.

DEMETRIUS.
Youngling, learn thou to make some meaner choice:
Lavina is thine elder brother's hope.

Youngster, learn to aim lower:
Lavinia is your older brother's target.

AARON.
Why, are ye mad, or know ye not in Rome
How furious and impatient they be,
And cannot brook competitors in love?
I tell you, lords, you do but plot your deaths
By this device.

What, are you mad, or don't you know how
angry and intolerant they are in Rome,
and won't tolerate rivals in love?
I tell you, my lords, this business
can only end in your deaths.

CHIRON.
Aaron, a thousand deaths
Would I propose to achieve her whom I love.

Aaron, I would die a thousand deaths
to get the one I love.

AARON.
To achieve her- how?

Get her how?

DEMETRIUS.
Why mak'st thou it so strange?
She is a woman, therefore may be woo'd;
She is a woman, therefore may be won;
She is Lavinia, therefore must be lov'd.
What, man! more water glideth by the mill
Than wots the miller of; and easy it is
Of a cut loaf to steal a shive, we know.
Though Bassianus be the Emperor's brother,

Why are you making such an issue of it?
She's a woman, so she can be wooed;
she's a woman, so she can be won;
she is Lavinia, so she must be loved.
What, man! There's more water goes past the mill
than the miller knows about, and it's easy
to steal a slice of a sliced loaf, that's obvious.
Although Bassanius is the brother of the Emperor,

Better than he have worn Vulcan's badge.

better men than him have been cheated.

AARON.
[Aside] Ay, and as good as Saturninus may.

Yes, and men as high as Saturnius could be.

DEMETRIUS.
Then why should he despair that knows to court it

Then why should a man give up hope when he knows how to woo

With words, fair looks, and liberality?
What, hast not thou full often struck a doe,
And borne her cleanly by the keeper's nose?

with words, good looks and generosity?
Haven't you ever shot a deer
and smuggled it out under the gamekeeper's nose?

AARON.
Why, then, it seems some certain snatch or so
Would serve your turns.

Why then, it seems that a quick bit of poaching would suit you.

CHIRON.
Ay, so the turn were served.

Yes, if that would do the job.

DEMETRIUS.
Aaron, thou hast hit it.

Aaron, you've hit the nail on the head.

AARON.
Would you had hit it too!
Then should not we be tir'd with this ado.
Why, hark ye, hark ye! and are you such fools
To square for this? Would it offend you, then,
That both should speed?

I wish you had too!
Then we wouldn't be bothered with all this fuss.
Now, listen here! Are you such idiots
that you fight over this? Would you mind
if both of you got what you wanted?

CHIRON.
Faith, not me.

I swear I wouldn't.

DEMETRIUS.
Nor me, so I were one.

Nor me, if it meant I got my share.

AARON.
For shame, be friends, and join for that you jar.

Then for heaven's sake be friends, and join forces to get the thing you're arguing over.

'Tis policy and stratagem must do
That you affect; and so must you resolve
That what you cannot as you would achieve,
You must perforce accomplish as you may.
Take this of me: Lucrece was not more chaste
Than this Lavinia, Bassianus' love.
A speedier course than ling'ring languishment
Must we pursue, and I have found the path.
My lords, a solemn hunting is in hand;

Planning and cunning must be used to get
what you want, and so you should resolve
that if you can't get what you want the way you want
you must get it any way you can.
Believe you me, Lucerece wasn't more chaste
than this Lavinia, the love of Bassanius.
We must follow a swifter plan than this
romantic meandering, and I know the way.
My lords, there is a ceremonial hunting trip under

There will the lovely Roman ladies troop;
The forest walks are wide and spacious,
And many unfrequented plots there are
Fitted by kind for rape and villainy.
Single you thither then this dainty doe,
And strike her home by force if not by words.

This way, or not at all, stand you in hope.
Come, come, our Empress, with her sacred wit
To villainy and vengeance consecrate,
Will we acquaint with all what we intend;
And she shall file our engines with advice
That will not suffer you to square yourselves,
But to your wishes' height advance you both.
The Emperor's court is like the house of Fame,
The palace full of tongues, of eyes, and ears;
The woods are ruthless, dreadful, deaf, and dull.
There speak and strike, brave boys, and take your turns;
There serve your lust, shadowed from heaven's eye,
And revel in Lavinia's treasury.

CHIRON.
Thy counsel, lad, smells of no cowardice.

DEMETRIUS.
Sit fas aut nefas, till I find the stream

To cool this heat, a charm to calm these fits,

Per Styga, per manes vehor.
Exeunt

way,
and the lovely Roman ladies will follow the hunt.
The paths in the forest are long and wide,
and there are many isolated spots
well suited to rape and villainy.
So isolate this dainty doe,
and get what you want with force, if words won't work;
this way is the only one for you.
Now look, our Empress, whose divine mind
is devoted to crime and revenge,
we will tell what we mean to do,
and she will refine our plans
so that you two won't have to quarrel
but get you both your hearts' desires.
The Emperor's court is like the house of Fame,
the palace is full of tongues, of eyes and ears;
the woods are pitiless, dreadful, deaf and dumb:
that's where you should speak and strike, brave lads, and take your turns;
let your lust run free there, out of sight of heaven,
and get your fill of Lavinia.

This is a brave plan, lad.

Whether it's right or wrong, until I can find the stream
which can cool this heat, some magic to calm my turmoil,
I am living in hell.

SCENE II. A forest near Rome

Enter TITUS ANDRONICUS, and his three sons, LUCIUS, QUINTUS, MARTIUS, making a noise with hounds and horns; and MARCUS

TITUS.
The hunt is up, the morn is bright and grey,
The fields are fragrant, and the woods are green.

The hunt has begun, the morning is bright and grey, the fields are sweet smelling and the woods are green.

Uncouple here, and let us make a bay,
And wake the Emperor and his lovely bride,
And rouse the Prince, and ring a hunter's peal,
That all the court may echo with the noise.
Sons, let it be your charge, as it is ours,
To attend the Emperor's person carefully.
I have been troubled in my sleep this night,
But dawning day new comfort hath inspir'd.
Here a cry of hounds, and wind horns in a peal.

Unleash the hounds and let's have a barking to wake the Emperor and his lovely bride, and wake the Prince, and blow a hunting horn, so that the whole court echoes with the noise. Sons, make it your duty, as I will, to guard the Emperor carefully. I had uneasy dreams last night, but the new morning has lifted my spirits.

Then enter SATURNINUS, TAMORA, BASSIANUS LAVINIA,
CHIRON, DEMETRIUS, and their attendants
Many good morrows to your Majesty!
Madam, to you as many and as good!
I promised your Grace a hunter's peal.

Many good mornings to your majesty; and the same to you madam, just as good. I promised your grace a hunting cry.

SATURNINUS.
And you have rung it lustily, my lords-
Somewhat too early for new-married ladies.

And you have given if lustily, my lords - a little too early for newly married ladies.

BASSIANUS.
Lavinia, how say you?

Lavinia, what do you say to that?

LAVINIA.
I say no;
I have been broad awake two hours and more.

I disagree; I've been wide awake for over two hours.

SATURNINUS.
Come on then, horse and chariots let us have,
And to our sport. [To TAMORA] Madam, now shall ye see
Our Roman hunting.

Come on then, let's get the horses and chariots, and get hunting. Madam, you shall now see how we Romans hunt.

MARCUS.
I have dogs, my lord,
Will rouse the proudest panther in the chase,
And climb the highest promontory top.

I have dogs, my lord, that will flush out the biggest panther, and climb the highest mountain.

TITUS.
And I have horse will follow where the game

Makes way, and run like swallows o'er the plain.

And I have horses that will follow wherever the quarry
bolts, and can run over the fields like swallows.

DEMETRIUS.
Chiron, we hunt not, we, with horse nor hound,
But hope to pluck a dainty doe to ground.
Exeunt

Chiron, we won't hunt with horses or hounds,
but hope we can bring down a dainty doe.

SCENE III. A lonely part of the forest

Enter AARON alone, with a bag of gold

AARON.
He that had wit would think that I had none,	*An intelligent man would think I was stupid,*
To bury so much gold under a tree	*burying so much gold under a tree*
And never after to inherit it.	*instead of enjoying the use of it.*
Let him that thinks of me so abjectly	*Let the one who thinks so poorly of me*
Know that this gold must coin a stratagem,	*know that this gold is part of a plan*
Which, cunningly effected, will beget	*which, executed with cunning, will cause*
A very excellent piece of villainy.	*an excellent bit of mischief.*
And so repose, sweet gold, for their unrest	*And so lie there, sweet gold, to cause trouble*
[Hides the gold]	*[Hides the gold]*
That have their alms out of the Empress' chest.	*to those who get their handouts from the Empress.*

Enter TAMORA alone, to the Moor

TAMORA.
My lovely Aaron, wherefore look'st thou sad	*My lovely Aaron, why do you look sad*
When everything does make a gleeful boast?	*when everything around is so happy?*
The birds chant melody on every bush;	*The birds are singing on every bush,*
The snakes lie rolled in the cheerful sun;	*the snakes lie coiled up in the warming sun,*
The green leaves quiver with the cooling wind	*the green leaves rustle in the cool breeze*
And make a chequer'd shadow on the ground;	*and make a dappled shadow on the ground.*
Under their sweet shade, Aaron, let us sit,	*Let's sit under their sweet shade, Aaron,*
And while the babbling echo mocks the hounds,	*and while the warbling echo copies the hounds,*
Replying shrilly to the well-tun'd horns,	*replying shrilly to be well tuned horns*
As if a double hunt were heard at once,	*as if two hunts were going on at the same time,*
Let us sit down and mark their yellowing noise;	*let's sit down and listen to their racket;*
And- after conflict such as was suppos'd	*and after we've enjoyed such a bout together*
The wand'ring prince and Dido once enjoyed,	*as Aeneas and Dido were supposed to have once enjoyed,*
When with a happy storm they were surpris'd,	*when they were caught out by a fortuitous storm*
And curtain'd with a counsel-keeping cave-	*which kept them hidden in a secret cave,*
We may, each wreathed in the other's arms,	*we may, wrapped in each other's arms,*
Our pastimes done, possess a golden slumber,	*our fun over, have a delicious sleep,*
Whiles hounds and horns and sweet melodious birds	*while the hounds and horns and sweet singing birds*
Be unto us as is a nurse's song	*will be like the song of a nurse to us,*
Of lullaby to bring her babe asleep.	*a lullaby to get her baby to sleep.*

AARON.
Madam, though Venus govern your desires,	*Madam, although your desires are ruled by Venus,*
Saturn is dominator over mine.	*Saturn is ruling over mine.*
What signifies my deadly-standing eye,	*What does my deathdealing eye signify,*
My silence and my cloudy melancholy,	*my silence and my dark brooding,*
My fleece of woolly hair that now uncurls	*my fleece of woolly hair that now uncurls*
Even as an adder when she doth unroll	*like an adder when she uncoils herself*

To do some fatal execution?
No, madam, these are no venereal signs.
Vengeance is in my heart, death in my hand,

Blood and revenge are hammering in my head.
Hark, Tamora, the empress of my soul,
Which never hopes more heaven than rests in thee-
This is the day of doom for Bassianus;
His Philomel must lose her tongue to-day,
Thy sons make pillage of her chastity,
And wash their hands in Bassianus' blood.
Seest thou this letter? Take it up, I pray thee,
And give the King this fatal-plotted scroll.
Now question me no more; we are espied.
Here comes a parcel of our hopeful booty,
Which dreads not yet their lives' destruction.

Enter BASSIANUS and LAVINIA
TAMORA. Ah, my sweet Moor, sweeter to me than life!

AARON.
No more, great Empress: Bassianus comes.
Be cross with him; and I'll go fetch thy sons

To back thy quarrels, whatsoe'er they be.

Exit

BASSIANUS.
Who have we here? Rome's royal Emperess,
Unfurnish'd of her well-beseeming troop?
Or is it Dian, habited like her,
Who hath abandoned her holy groves
To see the general hunting in this forest?

TAMORA.
Saucy controller of my private steps!
Had I the pow'r that some say Dian had,
Thy temples should be planted presently
With horns, as was Actaeon's; and the hounds
Should drive upon thy new-transformed limbs,
Unmannerly intruder as thou art!

LAVINIA.
Under your patience, gentle Emperess,
'Tis thought you have a goodly gift in horning,

to make a fatal attack?
No, madam, these are not signs of love;
I have vengeance in my heart, my hand is ready to kill,
blood and revenge are pounding in my head.
Listen, Tamora, the Empress of my soul,
which never hopes to find anything better than you,
this must be Bassianus' last day,
Lavinia must have her tongue cut out today,
your sons must rape her
and wash their hands in his blood.
Do you see this letter? Take it, please,
and give the King this scroll, which plots death.
Ask me no more questions: we have been spotted.
Here come our intended victims,
who are not yet in fear of their lives.

Oh, my sweet Moor, you are sweeter to me than life itself!

No more, great Empress: Bassianus is coming.
Be quarrelsome with him; and I'll go and bring your sons
to back you up in your arguments, whatever they are.

Who've we got here? The royal Empress of Rome,
without her suitable bodyguard?
Or is it Diana, dressed like her,
who has left her holy woods
to see everybody hunting in this forest?

Insolentsteward of my private affairs!
If I had the power that some say Diana had
you would shortly have horns on your forehead, like Actaeon had; and the hounds
would attack your newly changed body,
ill mannered intruder that you are!

If you'll excuse me, gentle Empress,
it's thought that you are good at putting the horns on

33

And to be doubted that your Moor and you
Are singled forth to try thy experiments.
Jove shield your husband from his hounds to-day!
'Tis pity they should take him for a stag.

people,
and I suspect that your Moor and you
have sneaked off to experiment in the matter.
May Jove protect your husband from his dogs today!
It would be a shame if they mistook him for a stag.

BASSIANUS.
Believe me, Queen, your swarth Cimmerian
Doth make your honour of his body's hue,
Spotted, detested, and abominable.
Why are you sequest'red from all your train,
Dismounted from your snow-white goodly steed,
And wand'red hither to an obscure plot,
Accompanied but with a barbarous Moor,
If foul desire had not conducted you?

Believe me, Queen, your dark friend
makes your honour the same colour as his body,
stained, hated and revolting.
Why are you separated from all your entourage,
dismounted from your splendid snow white horse,
and wandering here in this secret place,
only accompanied by a savage Moor,
if it isn't for the fact that foul desire led you here?

LAVINIA.
And, being intercepted in your sport,
Great reason that my noble lord be rated
For sauciness. I pray you let us hence,
And let her joy her raven-coloured love;
This valley fits the purpose passing well.

And, being interrupted in your games,
that's the reason that my noble Lord is chastised
for impertinence. Please, let's go away,
and let her get her fill of her dark lover;
this valley is pretty suitable for the purpose.

BASSIANUS.
The King my brother shall have notice of this.

My brother the King shall be told about this.

LAVINIA.
Ay, for these slips have made him noted long.

Yes, for this immorality has disgraced him for a long
time.

Good king, to be so mightily abused!

What a good king, that he should be so dreadfully
abused!

TAMORA.
Why, I have patience to endure all this.
Enter CHIRON and DEMETRIUS

Well, I can put up with this.

DEMETRIUS.
How now, dear sovereign, and our gracious mother!
Why doth your Highness look so pale and wan?

Hello, dear Queen, and our gracious mother!
Why does your Highness look so pale and sickly?

TAMORA.
Have I not reason, think you, to look pale?
These two have 'ticed me hither to this place.
A barren detested vale you see it is:
The trees, though summer, yet forlorn and lean,

Don't you think I have good reason to look pale?
These two have tricked me to this place:
you can see it's a horrible barren valley;
even though it's summer the trees are wasted and
thin,

Overcome with moss and baleful mistletoe;
Here never shines the sun; here nothing breeds,

overrun by moss and evil mistletoe;
the sun never shines here, nothing breeds here

Unless the nightly owl or fatal raven. | *unless it is the night owl and the ominous raven.*
And when they show'd me this abhorred pit, | *And when they showed me this revolting pit,*
They told me, here, at dead time of the night, | *they told me that here at the dead of night*
A thousand fiends, a thousand hissing snakes, | *a thousand daemons, a thousand hissing snakes,*
Ten thousand swelling toads, as many urchins, | *ten thousand swelling toads, the same number of goblins,*

Would make such fearful and confused cries | *would make such a devilish cacophony*
As any mortal body hearing it | *that any mortal person hearing it*
Should straight fall mad or else die suddenly. | *would become mad at once, or else suddenly die.*
No sooner had they told this hellish tale | *No sooner had they told me this awful tale*
But straight they told me they would bind me here | *then they told me that they would tie me here*
Unto the body of a dismal yew, | *to the trunk of a dismal yew tree*
And leave me to this miserable death. | *and leave me to this miserable death.*
And then they call'd me foul adulteress, | *And then they called me a foul adulteress,*
Lascivious Goth, and all the bitterest terms | *a lecherous Goth, and all themost horrible things*
That ever ear did hear to such effect; | *that you could possibly imagine.*
And had you not by wondrous fortune come, | *If you hadn't so luckily arrived*
This vengeance on me had they executed. | *they would have carried out this vengeance on me.*
Revenge it, as you love your mother's life, | *Revenge it out of love for your mother*
Or be ye not henceforth call'd my children. | *or you won't be called my children from now on.*

DEMETRIUS.
This is a witness that I am thy son. | *This proves that I am your son.*
[Stabs BASSIANUS]

CHIRON.
And this for me, struck home to show my strength. | *And the same for me, I strike to prove the strength of my love.*

[Also stabs]

LAVINIA.
Ay, come, Semiramis- nay, barbarous Tamora, | *Yes, come, Semiramis–no, savage Tamora,*
For no name fits thy nature but thy own! | *no name suits your evil but your own!*

TAMORA.
Give me the poniard; you shall know, my boys, | *Give me the dagger; you shall see, my boys,*
Your mother's hand shall right your mother's wrong. | *your mother shall revenge her wrongs with her own hands.*

DEMETRIUS.
Stay, madam, here is more belongs to her; | *Wait, madam, there is more to her than just her life;*
First thrash the corn, then after burn the straw. | *first we thresh the corn, then we burn the straw.*
This minion stood upon her chastity, | *This hussy was proud of her chastity,*
Upon her nuptial vow, her loyalty, | *her wedding vow, her loyalty,*
And with that quaint hope braves your mightiness; | *and with that old-fashioned nonsense tried to face down your magnificence;*

And shall she carry this unto her grave? | *are we going to let her take that to her grave?*

CHIRON.
An if she do, I would I were an eunuch.
Drag hence her husband to some secret hole,
And make his dead trunk pillow to our lust.

May I be a eunuch if she does.
Drag her husband to some secret hollow,
and his body can be the bed for our games.

TAMORA.
But when ye have the honey we desire,
Let not this wasp outlive, us both to sting.

But when you have the honey you want
don't let this wasp stay alive to sting us both.

CHIRON.
I warrant you, madam, we will make that sure.
Come, mistress, now perforce we will enjoy
That nice-preserved honesty of yours.

I promise you, madam, will make certain of that.
Come, mistress, we shall now enjoy by force
that chastity you were so proud of.

LAVINIA.
O Tamora! thou bearest a woman's face-

Oh Tamora! You have a woman's face–

TAMORA.
I will not hear her speak; away with her!

I won't listen to her; take away!

LAVINIA.
Sweet lords, entreat her hear me but a word.

Sweet lords, please ask her to just listen to a word
from me.

DEMETRIUS.
Listen, fair madam: let it be your glory
To see her tears; but be your heart to them
As unrelenting flint to drops of rain.

Listen, fair madam: take pride
in causing her tears; but let them affect your heart
no more than the hard flint is affected by raindrops.

LAVINIA.
When did the tiger's young ones teach the dam?
O, do not learn her wrath- she taught it thee;
The milk thou suck'dst from her did turn to marble,
Even at thy teat thou hadst thy tyranny.
Yet every mother breeds not sons alike:
[To CHIRON] Do thou entreat her show a
woman's pity.
CHIRON.
What, wouldst thou have me prove myself a bastard?

When did the tiger cubs teach their mother?
Don't teach her hatred–she taught it to you;
the milk you sucked from her turned to marble,
even in your infancy you became evil.
But not every son is like his mother:
ask her to show a woman's pity.

What, you want me to show that I am a bastard?

LAVINIA.
'Tis true, the raven doth not hatch a lark.
Yet have I heard- O, could I find it now!-
The lion, mov'd with pity, did endure
To have his princely paws par'd all away.
Some say that ravens foster forlorn children,
The whilst their own birds famish in their nests;

Its true, ravens don't give birth to larks.
But I have heard–oh if it could happen now!–
That the lion, when moved by pity, allowed
himself to put away his princely claws.
Some say the ravens raise lost children,
while their own chicks starve in their nests;

O, be to me, though thy hard heart say no,

Nothing so kind, but something pitiful!

TAMORA.
I know not what it means; away with her!

LAVINIA.
O, let me teach thee! For my father's sake,
That gave thee life when well he might have slain thee,
Be not obdurate, open thy deaf ears.

TAMORA.
Hadst thou in person ne'er offended me,
Even for his sake am I pitiless.
Remember, boys, I pour'd forth tears in vain
To save your brother from the sacrifice;

But fierce Andronicus would not relent.
Therefore away with her, and use her as you will;
The worse to her the better lov'd of me.

LAVINIA.
O Tamora, be call'd a gentle queen,
And with thine own hands kill me in this place!
For 'tis not life that I have begg'd so long;
Poor I was slain when Bassianus died.

TAMORA.
What beg'st thou, then? Fond woman, let me go.

LAVINIA.
'Tis present death I beg; and one thing more,
That womanhood denies my tongue to tell:
O, keep me from their worse than killing lust,

And tumble me into some loathsome pit,
Where never man's eye may behold my body;
Do this, and be a charitable murderer.

TAMORA.
So should I rob my sweet sons of their fee;
No, let them satisfy their lust on thee.

DEMETRIUS.
Away! for thou hast stay'd us here too long.

---

you don't have to be as kind to me, but please show me pity,
even if your hard heart is telling you not to.

I don't know what she's talking about; take her away!

Oh, let me teach you! For the sake of my father,
who let you live when he could have killed you,

don't be stubborn, open your deaf ears.

If you personally had never offended me,
I am pitiless for his sake.
Remember, boys, I cried floods of tears
in a vain attempt to save your brother from being sacrificed;
But savage Andronicus would not relent.
So take away, and do what you want with her;
the worse you treat her the better I'll like it.

Oh Tamora, be called a kind Queen,
and kill me here with your own hands!
It's not life I have been begging for for so long;
I was as good as dead when Bassianus died.

What are you begging for then? Foolish woman, let me go.

I'm begging for instant death; and another thing,
that my womanhood forbids me from speaking:
oh, save me from their lust which is worse than death,
and throw me into some horrid pit,
where no man can ever look at my body;
do this, and be a kind murderer.

That would rob my sweet sons of their rewards;
no, let them satisfy their lusts with you.

Let's go! You have kept us here too long.

LAVINIA.
No grace? no womanhood? Ah, beastly creature,

The blot and enemy to our general name!
Confusion fall-

No kindness? No womanhood? Oh you horrible creature,
a stain on the reputation of womankind!

CHIRON.
Nay, then I'll stop your mouth. Bring thou her husband.
This is the hole where Aaron bid us hide him.
DEMETRIUS throws the body
of BASSIANUS into the pit; then exeunt
DEMETRIUS and CHIRON, dragging off LAVINIA

Right, I'll shut your mouth. You bring her husband.
This is the hole where Aaron told us to hide him.

TAMORA.
Farewell, my sons; see that you make her sure.

Ne'er let my heart know merry cheer indeed
Till all the Andronici be made away.
Now will I hence to seek my lovely Moor,
And let my spleenful sons this trull deflower.

Goodbye, my sons; make sure she can't give anything away.
May my heart never be happy
until all the family of Andronicus are finished.
Now I will go and find my lovely Moor,
and let my vicious sons deflower this slut.

Exit
Re-enter AARON, with two
of TITUS' sons, QUINTUS and MARTIUS

AARON.
Come on, my lords, the better foot before;
Straight will I bring you to the loathsome pit
Where I espied the panther fast asleep.

Come on, my lords, best foot forward;
I'll bring you straight to the horrible pit
where I saw the panther fast asleep.

QUINTUS.
My sight is very dull, whate'er it bodes.

My sight feels very cloudy, whatever that means.

MARTIUS.
And mine, I promise you; were it not for shame,

Well could I leave our sport to sleep awhile.
[Falls into the pit]

And mine, I can tell you; if it wasn't that I would be embarrassed
I could easily leave the hunt to have a little sleep.

QUINTUS.
What, art thou fallen? What subtle hole is this,
Whose mouth is covered with rude-growing briers,
Upon whose leaves are drops of new-shed blood

As fresh as morning dew distill'd on flowers?
A very fatal place it seems to me.

What, have you fallen? What cunning hole is this,
whose mouth is covered with rough brambles,
whose leaves are covered with drops of newly shed blood
as fresh as the morning dew settling on the flowers?
It seems a very deadly place to me.

Speak, brother, hast thou hurt thee with the fall?

Speak to me, brother, have you hurt yourself in falling?

MARTIUS.
O brother, with the dismal'st object hurt
That ever eye with sight made heart lament!

O brother, I have been hurt by the most dismal thing that was ever seen to make the heart grieve.

AARON.
[Aside] Now will I fetch the King to find them here,
That he thereby may have a likely guess
How these were they that made away his brother.
Exit

Now I'll bring the king here to find them, so that he will think it's probable that they were the ones who killed his brother.

MARTIUS.
Why dost not comfort me, and help me out
From this unhallow'd and blood-stained hole?

Why don't you assist me and help me out of this devilish bloodstained hole?

QUINTUS.
I am surprised with an uncouth fear;
A chilling sweat o'er-runs my trembling joints;
My heart suspects more than mine eye can see.

I am bewildered by a strange fear; a cold sweat runs over my trembling limbs; my heart suspects there is more to this than meets the eye.

MARTIUS.
To prove thou hast a true divining heart,
Aaron and thou look down into this den,
And see a fearful sight of blood and death.

To prove these suspicions of your heart are correct, you and Aaron should look down into this pit, and see a terrible vision of blood and death.

QUINTUS.
Aaron is gone, and my compassionate heart
Will not permit mine eyes once to behold
The thing whereat it trembles by surmise;
O, tell me who it is, for ne'er till now
Was I a child to fear I know not what.

Aaron has gone, and my sorrowing heart will not allow my eyes to look at the thing it fearfully thinks is there; oh, tell me who it is, for never before have I suffered such a nameless fear.

MARTIUS.
Lord Bassianus lies beray'd in blood,
All on a heap, like to a slaughtered lamb,
In this detested, dark, blood-drinking pit.

Lord Bassianus lies covered in blood, all in a heap, like a slaughtered lamb, in this foul, dark, blood drinking pit.

QUINTUS.
If it be dark, how dost thou know 'tis he?

If it's dark, how do you know it's him?

MARTIUS.
Upon his bloody finger he doth wear
A precious ring that lightens all this hole,
Which, like a taper in some monument,

On his bloody finger he is wearing a precious ring that lights up this pit, which, like a lighted candle on a tomb,

Doth shine upon the dead man's earthy cheeks,
And shows the ragged entrails of this pit;
So pale did shine the moon on Pyramus
When he by night lay bath'd in maiden blood.
O brother, help me with thy fainting hand-
If fear hath made thee faint, as me it hath-
Out of this fell devouring receptacle,
As hateful as Cocytus' misty mouth.

*shines on the dead man's pale cheeks,
and shows the rough insides of this hole.
This is how the pale moon shone on Pyramus
when he lay in the night bathed in maiden's blood.
O brother, help me with your trembling hand—
if fear has made you tremble, as it has me—
out of this horrible swallowing place,
as revolting as the mouth of hell.*

QUINTUS.
Reach me thy hand, that I may help thee out,
Or, wanting strength to do thee so much good,
I may be pluck'd into the swallowing womb
Of this deep pit, poor Bassianus' grave.
I have no strength to pluck thee to the brink.

*Give me your hand so I can help you out,
or, if I don't have the strength to help you,
I may be pulled down into the devouring womb
of this deep pit, the grave of poor Bassianus.*

MARTIUS.
Nor I no strength to climb without thy help.

*I don't have the strength to climb out without your
help.*

QUINTUS.
Thy hand once more; I will not loose again,
Till thou art here aloft, or I below.
Thou canst not come to me- I come to thee. [Falls in]

*Give me your hand again; I won't let go again
until you're up here, or I'm down there.
You can't come up to me—I'm coming down to you.*

Enter the EMPEROR and AARON the Moor
SATURNINUS. Along with me! I'll see what hole
is here,
And what he is that now is leapt into it.
Say, who art thou that lately didst descend
Into this gaping hollow of the earth?

*Follow me! I'll see what this pit is,
and who that is who just leapt into it.
Speak, who are you who just went in
to this hollow in the earth?*

MARTIUS.
The unhappy sons of old Andronicus,
Brought hither in a most unlucky hour,
To find thy brother Bassianus dead.

*The unfortunate sons of old Andronicus,
brought here at a very unlucky time,
to find your brother Bassianus dead.*

SATURNINUS.
My brother dead! I know thou dost but jest:
He and his lady both are at the lodge
Upon the north side of this pleasant chase;

'Tis not an hour since I left them there.

*My brother dead! I know you're only joking:
he and his lady are both at the lodge
on the north side of this pleasant hunting
ground;
I left them there less than an hour ago.*

MARTIUS.
We know not where you left them all alive;
But, out alas! here have we found him dead.
 Re-enter TAMORA, with

*We don't know where you left them alive;
but now alas we have found him here dead.*

attendants; TITUS ANDRONICUS and Lucius

TAMORA.
Where is my lord the King?

Where is my lord the King?

SATURNINUS.
Here, Tamora; though griev'd with killing grief.

Here, Tamora; though I am saddened with deadly grief.

TAMORA.
Where is thy brother Bassianus?

Where is your brother Bassianus?

SATURNINUS.
Now to the bottom dost thou search my wound;
Poor Bassianus here lies murdered.

*Now you're probing my wound to its depths;
poor Bassianus is lying here murdered.*

TAMORA.
Then all too late I bring this fatal writ,
The complot of this timeless tragedy;

And wonder greatly that man's face can fold
In pleasing smiles such murderous tyranny.
 [She giveth SATURNINE a letter]

*Then I have brought this fatal paper too late,
which shows the conspiracy which caused this
untimely tragedy;
and I'm amazed that a man's face can hide
such murderous evil behind sweet smiles.*

SATURNINUS.
[Reads] 'An if we miss to meet him handsomely,
Sweet huntsman- Bassianus 'tis we mean-
Do thou so much as dig the grave for him.
Thou know'st our meaning. Look for thy reward
Among the nettles at the elder-tree
Which overshades the mouth of that same pit
Where we decreed to bury Bassianus.
Do this, and purchase us thy lasting friends.'
O Tamora! was ever heard the like?
This is the pit and this the elder-tree.
Look, sirs, if you can find the huntsman out
That should have murdered Bassianus here.

*'And if we don't run across him,
sweet huntsman–we mean Bassianus–
then you should dig a grave for him.
You know what I mean. Look for your reward
amongst the nettles at the foot of the elderberry tree
which hangs over the mouth of the same pit
where we have decided to bury Bassianus.
Do this, and win our eternal friendship.'
Oh Tamora! Did you ever hear anything like it?
Here is the pit and here is the elderberry tree.
Sirs, try and discover the huntsman
who would've murdered Bassianus here.*

AARON.
My gracious lord, here is the bag of gold.

My gracious lord, here is the bag of gold.

SATURNINUS.
[To TITUS] Two of thy whelps, fell curs of bloody kind,
Have here bereft my brother of his life.
Sirs, drag them from the pit unto the prison;

There let them bide until we have devis'd

*Two of your puppies, disgusting bloody curs,

have taken my brother's life here.
Gentlemen, drag them out of the pit and take them to the prison;
let them stay there until I have invented*

41

Some never-heard-of torturing pain for them.

some unprecedented form of torture for them.

TAMORA.
What, are they in this pit? O wondrous thing!
How easily murder is discovered!

What, are they in this pit? How amazing!
How easily murder is found out!

TITUS.
High Emperor, upon my feeble knee
I beg this boon, with tears not lightly shed,
That this fell fault of my accursed sons-
Accursed if the fault be prov'd in them-

High Emperor, on my weak knees
I beg this favour, with tears I don't shed lightly:
that this terrible crime of my accursed sons—
accursed if they are proved to have committed the
crime—

SATURNINUS.
If it be prov'd! You see it is apparent.
Who found this letter? Tamora, was it you?

If it is proved! You can see it is obvious.
Who found this letter? Tamora, was it you?

TAMORA.
Andronicus himself did take it up.

Andronicus himself picked it up.

TITUS.
I did, my lord, yet let me be their bail;
For, by my fathers' reverend tomb, I vow
They shall be ready at your Highness' will
To answer their suspicion with their lives.

I did, my lord, but let me stand bail for them;
I swear by the sacred tomb of my fathers
that they shall be ready when your Highness desires
to answer with their lives if they are guilty.

SATURNINUS.
Thou shalt not bail them; see thou follow me.

You will not stand bail for them; make sure you
follow me.

Some bring the murdered body, some the murderers;

Some of you bring the murdered body, some bring
the murderers;

Let them not speak a word- the guilt is plain;
For, by my soul, were there worse end than death,
That end upon them should be executed.

don't let them speak a word–their guilt is obvious;
I swear, if there was a worse thing than death
I would give it to them.

TAMORA.
Andronicus, I will entreat the King.
Fear not thy sons; they shall do well enough.

Andronicus, I will plead your case to the King.
Don't worry for your sons; they will be all right.

TITUS.
Come, Lucius, come; stay not to talk with them.
Exeunt

Come on, Lucius, come; don't stop to talk with them.

SCENE IV. Another part of the forest

Enter the Empress' sons, DEMETRIUS and CHIRON, with LAVINIA, her hands cut off, and her tongue cut out, and ravish'd

DEMETRIUS.
So, now go tell, an if thy tongue can speak,
Who 'twas that cut thy tongue and ravish'd thee.

So, now go and tell tales, if your tongue can speak,
tell them who cut your tongue out and raped you.

CHIRON.
Write down thy mind, bewray thy meaning so,

An if thy stumps will let thee play the scribe.

Write down what's in your mind, show your meaning that way,
if your stumps will let you hold a pen.

DEMETRIUS.
See how with signs and tokens she can scrawl.

Let's see what scribbles she can manage.

CHIRON.
Go home, call for sweet water, wash thy hands.

Go home, call for rose water, wash your hands.

DEMETRIUS.
She hath no tongue to call, nor hands to wash;
And so let's leave her to her silent walks.

She has no tongue to call with, nor hands to wash;
and so let's leave her to her silent stroll.

CHIRON.
An 'twere my cause, I should go hang myself.

If I were in her place, I would hang myself.

DEMETRIUS.
If thou hadst hands to help thee knit the cord.
Exeunt DEMETRIUS and CHIRON

If you had hands to help you tie the knot.

Wind horns. Enter MARCUS, from hunting
MARCUS. Who is this?- my niece, that flies away so fast?
Cousin, a word: where is your husband?
If I do dream, would all my wealth would wake me!
If I do wake, some planet strike me down,
That I may slumber an eternal sleep!
Speak, gentle niece. What stern ungentle hands
Hath lopp'd, and hew'd, and made thy body bare
Of her two branches- those sweet ornaments
Whose circling shadows kings have sought to sleep in,
And might not gain so great a happiness
As half thy love? Why dost not speak to me?

Who's this? Is this my niece, running away so fast?
Cousin, let me have a word: where is your husband?
If I'm dreaming, I'd give all my wealth to wake up!
If I'm awake, may some planet strike me down,
so I can rest in eternal sleep!
Speak, gentle niece. What harsh rough hands
have chopped and hacked and stripped your body
of your arms–those sweet ornaments
which kings have wished to be hugged by,

thinking it would be the greatest happiness
to have only half your love? Why don't you speak to me?

Alas, a crimson river of warm blood,
Like to a bubbling fountain stirr'd with wind,
Doth rise and fall between thy rosed lips,
Coming and going with thy honey breath.
But sure some Tereus hath deflowered thee,
And, lest thou shouldst detect him, cut thy tongue.

Ah, now thou turn'st away thy face for shame!
And notwithstanding all this loss of blood-
As from a conduit with three issuing spouts-
Yet do thy cheeks look red as Titan's face
Blushing to be encount'red with a cloud.
Shall I speak for thee? Shall I say 'tis so?

O, that I knew thy heart, and knew the beast,

That I might rail at him to ease my mind!
Sorrow concealed, like an oven stopp'd,
Doth burn the heart to cinders where it is.
Fair Philomel, why she but lost her tongue,
And in a tedious sampler sew'd her mind;

But, lovely niece, that mean is cut from thee.
A craftier Tereus, cousin, hast thou met,
And he hath cut those pretty fingers off
That could have better sew'd than Philomel.
O, had the monster seen those lily hands
Tremble like aspen leaves upon a lute
And make the silken strings delight to kiss them,
He would not then have touch'd them for his life!
Or had he heard the heavenly harmony
Which that sweet tongue hath made,
He would have dropp'd his knife, and fell asleep,
As Cerberus at the Thracian poet's feet.
Come, let us go, and make thy father blind,
For such a sight will blind a father's eye;
One hour's storm will drown the fragrant meads,
What will whole months of tears thy father's eyes?

Do not draw back, for we will mourn with thee;
O, could our mourning case thy misery!
Exeunt

Alas, a red river of warm blood,
like a bubbling fountain blown by the wind,
is rising and falling between your rosy lips,
coming and going with your sweet breath.
It's obvious some rapist has deflowered you,
and, in case you would expose him, cut out your tongue.

Ah, now you turn your face away in shame!
And despite all this loss of blood–
flowing like a fountain with three spouts–
your cheeks look as red as the face of the sun,
blushing to be covered with a cloud.
Shall I speak for you? Shall I say this is what happened?
Oh, if only I knew what was inside, and knew the animal who did this,
so I could attack him to ease my pain!
Hidden sorrow, like an oven with its doors closed,
Burns the heart to cinders inside.
Fair Philomel only lost her tongue,
and with laborious embroidery sewed out her message;
but, lovely niece, that method is denied you.
You have met a craftier rapist, cousin,
and he has cut off those pretty fingers
which could have sewed better than Philomel.
Oh, if the monster had seen those white hands
trembling like the leaves of an aspen on a lute
making the silken strings delighted to be touched,
he would not have touched them for his life!
Or if he had heard the heavenly music
which your sweet tongue has made,
he would have dropped his knife and fallen asleep
like Cerberus enchanted by Orpheus.
Come, let us go, and make your father blind,
for such sight will blind a father's eyes;
One hour of storms can flood the fragrant meadows,
what will whole months of tears do to your father's eyes!
Don't back away, we will mourn with you;
if only our mourning could ease your misery!

ACT III

SCENE I. Rome. A street

Enter the JUDGES, TRIBUNES, and SENATORS, with TITUS' two sons
MARTIUS and QUINTUS bound, passing on the stage to the place of
execution, and TITUS going before, pleading

TITUS.
Hear me, grave fathers; noble Tribunes, stay!
For pity of mine age, whose youth was spent

In dangerous wars whilst you securely slept;
For all my blood in Rome's great quarrel shed,
For all the frosty nights that I have watch'd,
And for these bitter tears, which now you see
Filling the aged wrinkles in my cheeks,
Be pitiful to my condemned sons,
Whose souls are not corrupted as 'tis thought.
For two and twenty sons I never wept,
Because they died in honour's lofty bed.
[ANDRONICUS lieth down, and the judges
 pass by him with the prisoners, and exeunt]
For these, Tribunes, in the dust I write
My heart's deep languor and my soul's sad tears.
Let my tears stanch the earth's dry appetite;
My sons' sweet blood will make it shame and blush.

O earth, I will befriend thee more with rain
That shall distil from these two ancient urns,
Than youthful April shall with all his show'rs.
In summer's drought I'll drop upon thee still;
In winter with warm tears I'll melt the snow
And keep eternal spring-time on thy face,
So thou refuse to drink my dear sons' blood.
Enter Lucius with his weapon drawn
O reverend Tribunes! O gentle aged men!
Unbind my sons, reverse the doom of death,
And let me say, that never wept before,
My tears are now prevailing orators.

LUCIUS.
O noble father, you lament in vain;
The Tribunes hear you not, no man is by,
And you recount your sorrows to a stone.

TITUS.
Ah, Lucius, for thy brothers let me plead!
Grave Tribunes, once more I entreat of you.

Hear me, revered fathers; noble Tribunes, wait!
Out of pity for my age, the age of one whose youth
was spent
fighting dangerous wars whilst you slept in safety;
for all the blood I shed in Rome's great cause,
for all the frosty nights I have stayed awake,
and for these bitter tears, which you can now see,
filling the wrinkles of age in my cheeks,
be merciful to my condemned sons,
whose souls are not as evil as is supposed.
I never wept for the twenty two sons I have lost,
because they died honourable deaths.

Tribunes, I'm writing the great sorrows of my heart
in the dust with the sad tears of my soul.
Let my tears satisfy the needs of the dry earth,
for my sons' sweet blood will shame it and make it
blush.
Oh earth, I will give you more rain
from these two ancient vessels,
than you will ever get from April's showers.
In the droughts of summer I'll still water you;
in winter I'll melt the snow with warm tears
and give your surface eternal spring,
as long as you refuse to drink my sons' blood.

Oh reverend Tribunes! Oh you kind old men!
Release my sons, reverse the death sentence,
and let me, who has never cried before, know
that my tears are successful pleaders.

Oh noble father, you plead in vain;
the Tribunes can't hear you, there's no-one here,
and you are telling your sorrows to stone.

Ah, Lucius, let me beg for your brothers!
Great Tribunes, I beg you once again.

47

LUCIUS.
My gracious lord, no tribune hears you speak.

My gracious lord, no tribune is listening.

TITUS.
Why, 'tis no matter, man: if they did hear,
They would not mark me; if they did mark,
They would not pity me; yet plead I must,
And bootless unto them.
Therefore I tell my sorrows to the stones;
Who though they cannot answer my distress,
Yet in some sort they are better than the Tribunes,
For that they will not intercept my tale.
When I do weep, they humbly at my feet
Receive my tears, and seem to weep with me;
And were they but attired in grave weeds,
Rome could afford no tribunes like to these.
A stone is soft as wax: tribunes more hard than stones.
A stone is silent and offendeth not,
And tribunes with their tongues doom men to death.

It doesn't matter, man; if they heard me
they wouldn't pay attention; if they paid attention
they wouldn't pity me; but I must beg
even when it's useless.
So I will tell my sorrows to the stones;
though they can't respond to my distress
in some ways they are better than the Tribunes,
because they won't interrupt me.
When I weep they humbly, around my feet,
receive my tears, and seem to be weeping with me;
if they were just dressed in solemn robes
Rome could have no better tribunes than these.
Stones are soft as wax, compared to tribunes
who are hard as stones.
Stones are silent and do no harm,
while tribunes use their tongues to condemn men to death.

[Rises]
But wherefore stand'st thou with thy weapon drawn?

But why are you standing with your sword out?

LUCIUS.
To rescue my two brothers from their death;
For which attempt the judges have pronounc'd
My everlasting doom of banishment.

To rescue my two brothers from their death;
the judges have announced that
I will be permanently exiled for this.

TITUS.
O happy man! they have befriended thee.
Why, foolish Lucius, dost thou not perceive
That Rome is but a wilderness of tigers?
Tigers must prey, and Rome affords no prey
But me and mine; how happy art thou then
From these devourers to be banished!
But who comes with our brother Marcus here?

You happy man! They've done you a favour.
Why, foolish Lucius, can't you see
that Rome is just a desert full of tigers?
Tigers must hunt, and Rome has no prey
except for me and my family; how lucky you are
to be sent away from these beasts!
But who is this who comes here with our brother Marcus?

Enter MARCUS with LAVINIA

MARCUS.
Titus, prepare thy aged eyes to weep,
Or if not so, thy noble heart to break.
I bring consuming sorrow to thine age.

Titus, get ready for your old eyes to weep,
or if not for your noble heart to break.
I'm bringing overwhelming sorrow to your old age.

TITUS.

48

Will it consume me? Let me see it then.

Will it overwhelm me? Then give it to me.

MARCUS.
This was thy daughter.

This was your daughter.

TITUS.
Why, Marcus, so she is.

Why, Marcus, she still is.

LUCIUS.
Ay me! this object kills me.

Alas! this is killing me.

TITUS.
Faint-hearted boy, arise, and look upon her.
Speak, Lavinia, what accursed hand
Hath made thee handless in thy father's sight?
What fool hath added water to the sea,
Or brought a fagot to bright-burning Troy?
My grief was at the height before thou cam'st,
And now like Nilus it disdaineth bounds.
Give me a sword, I'll chop off my hands too,
For they have fought for Rome, and all in vain;
And they have nurs'd this woe in feeding life;
In bootless prayer have they been held up,
And they have serv'd me to effectless use.
Now all the service I require of them
Is that the one will help to cut the other.
'Tis well, Lavinia, that thou hast no hands;
For hands to do Rome service is but vain.

Fainthearted boy, get up and look at her.
Speak, Lavinia, what cursed hand
has made your father see you have no hands?
What fool has added a drop of water to the sea,
or tossed a twig on the fire of Troy?
My grief was at its height before you came,
and now, like the Nile, it floods everywhere.
Give me a sword, I'll chop my hands off too,
because they have fought for Rome without reward;
they have helped this sorrow by keeping me alive;
they have been held up in unanswered prayers,
and everything they have done has been useless.
Now all I ask them to do
is for one to help cut off the other.
It's good, Lavinia, that you have no hands,
for it's useless to have hands if they serve Rome.

LUCIUS.
Speak, gentle sister, who hath martyr'd thee?

Speak, gentle sister, who has tortured you?

MARCUS.
O, that delightful engine of her thoughts

That blabb'd them with such pleasing eloquence
Is torn from forth that pretty hollow cage,
Where like a sweet melodious bird it sung
Sweet varied notes, enchanting every ear!

Oh, that delightful tool she used to express her thoughts,
that chattered them with such delightful eloquence,
has been torn out of that pretty hollow cage
where it sang like a sweet tuneful bird
with lovely varied notes, enchanting everyone who heard!

LUCIUS.
O, say thou for her, who hath done this deed?

You speak for her, who did this?

MARCUS.
O, thus I found her straying in the park,
Seeking to hide herself as doth the deer
That hath receiv'd some unrecuring wound.

I found her wandering like this in the park,
trying to hide herself like a deer
that has been given an incurable wound.

TITUS.

It was my dear, and he that wounded her
Hath hurt me more than had he kill'd me dead;
For now I stand as one upon a rock,
Environ'd with a wilderness of sea,
Who marks the waxing tide grow wave by wave,
Expecting ever when some envious surge
Will in his brinish bowels swallow him.
This way to death my wretched sons are gone;
Here stands my other son, a banish'd man,
And here my brother, weeping at my woes.
But that which gives my soul the greatest spurn
Is dear Lavinia, dearer than my soul.
Had I but seen thy picture in this plight,
It would have madded me; what shall I do
Now I behold thy lively body so?
Thou hast no hands to wipe away thy tears,
Nor tongue to tell me who hath martyr'd thee;
Thy husband he is dead, and for his death
Thy brothers are condemn'd, and dead by this.
Look, Marcus! Ah, son Lucius, look on her!
When I did name her brothers, then fresh tears
Stood on her cheeks, as doth the honey dew
Upon a gath'red lily almost withered.

MARCUS.

Perchance she weeps because they kill'd her husband;
Perchance because she knows them innocent.

TITUS.

If they did kill thy husband, then be joyful,
Because the law hath ta'en revenge on them.
No, no, they would not do so foul a deed;
Witness the sorrow that their sister makes.
Gentle Lavinia, let me kiss thy lips,
Or make some sign how I may do thee ease.
Shall thy good uncle and thy brother Lucius
And thou and I sit round about some fountain,
Looking all downwards to behold our cheeks
How they are stain'd, like meadows yet not dry
With miry slime left on them by a flood?
And in the fountain shall we gaze so long,
Till the fresh taste be taken from that clearness,
And made a brine-pit with our bitter tears?

Or shall we cut away our hands like thine?

*She was my darling, and whoever harmed her
has hurt me more than if he had killed me;
Now I'm like a man standing on a rock,
surrounded by a wild sea,
watching the tide coming in wave after wave,
always expecting that some great surge
will swallow him up into its salty depths.
My wretched sons have gone that way to death;
here is my other son, an exile,
and here is my brother, weeping at my sorrow.
But the thing which stabs me to the heart
is dear Lavinia, dearer to me than myself.
If I had just seen a picture of you in this state
it would have driven me mad; what will happen
now I see your living body like this?
You have no hands to wipe away your tears,
and no tongue to tell me who tortured you;
your husband is dead, and your brothers are
condemned to death for his death.
Look, Marcus! Ah, Lucius, my son, look at her!
When I spoke of her brothers fresh tears
fell on her cheeks, like sweet dew falls
on a picked lily which is almost dead.*

*Maybe she weeps because they killed her husband,

or maybe because she knows they are innocent.*

*If they did kill your husband, then be happy,
because the law has punished them.
No, no, they would not do such an awful thing;
see how sad their sister is.
Gentle Lavinia, let me kiss your lips,
or give me some sign of how I can help you.
Shall your good uncle and your brother Lucius
and you and I sit round some fountain,
all looking downwards to see how our cheeks
are stained, like meadows that haven't dried
after a flood, with the muddy slime still on them.
And shall we gaze into that fountain for so long,
until the fresh sweetness has gone from it
and it's been turned into a salt pit by our bitter
tears?
Or shall we bite off our tongues, and spend the rest*

Or shall we bite our tongues, and in dumb shows
Pass the remainder of our hateful days?
What shall we do? Let us that have our tongues

Plot some device of further misery
To make us wonder'd at in time to come.

of our awful lives in dumb show?

What shall we do? Let those of us who still have tongues
plot some further deadly plan
which will amaze the ones who come after us.

LUCIUS.
Sweet father, cease your tears; for at your grief
See how my wretched sister sobs and weeps.

Sweet father, stop crying; look how my wretched
sister sobs and weeps at your grief.

MARCUS.
Patience, dear niece. Good Titus, dry thine eyes.

Be calm, dear niece. Good Titus, dry your eyes.

TITUS.
Ah, Marcus, Marcus! Brother, well I wot
Thy napkin cannot drink a tear of mine,
For thou, poor man, hast drown'd it with thine own.

Ah, Marcus, Marcus! Brother, I well know
that your handkerchief can't soak up any of my tears,
because, poor man, it's sodden with your own.

LUCIUS.
Ah, my Lavinia, I will wipe thy cheeks.

Ah, my Lavinia, let me wipe your cheeks.

TITUS.
Mark, Marcus, mark! I understand her signs.
Had she a tongue to speak, now would she say
That to her brother which I said to thee:
His napkin, with his true tears all bewet,
Can do no service on her sorrowful cheeks.
O, what a sympathy of woe is this
As far from help as Limbo is from bliss!
Enter AARON the Moor

Look, Marcus, look! I can understand her signs.
If she had a tongue to speak, she would say
to her brother what I just said to you:
his handkerchief, soaked with his true tears,
can't help to dry her sorrowful cheeks.
What an outpouring of sorrow this is,
as far from help as hell is from heaven!

AARON.
Titus Andronicus, my lord the Emperor
Sends thee this word, that, if thou love thy sons,
Let Marcus, Lucius, or thyself, old Titus,
Or any one of you, chop off your hand
And send it to the King: he for the same
Will send thee hither both thy sons alive,
And that shall be the ransom for their fault.

Titus Andronicus, my lord the Emperor
sends you this message, that if you love your sons
let Marcus, or Lucius, or yourself, old Titus,
any one of you, chop off your hand
and send it to the King: in return
he will send you both your sons alive,
and that will pay for their crime.

TITUS.
O gracious Emperor! O gentle Aaron!
Did ever raven sing so like a lark
That gives sweet tidings of the sun's uprise?
With all my heart I'll send the Emperor my hand.
Good Aaron, wilt thou help to chop it off?

Oh gracious Emperor! Oh gentle Aaron!
Did a raven ever sing so like a lark,
giving sweet tidings of the sunrise?
I'll very gladly send the Emperor my hand.
Good Aaron, will you help me chop it off?

LUCIUS.
Stay, father! for that noble hand of thine,
That hath thrown down so many enemies,
Shall not be sent. My hand will serve the turn,
My youth can better spare my blood than you,

And therefore mine shall save my brothers' lives.

Wait, father! That noble hand of yours,
which has defeated so many enemies,
will not be sent. My hand will do the job,
as I'm young and can stand the blood loss better
than you,
and so mine will save my brothers' lives.

MARCUS.
Which of your hands hath not defended Rome
And rear'd aloft the bloody battle-axe,
Writing destruction on the enemy's castle?
O, none of both but are of high desert!
My hand hath been but idle; let it serve
To ransom my two nephews from their death;
Then have I kept it to a worthy end.

Which of your hands hasn't defended Rome
and lifted up the bloody battleaxe,
smashing down the enemy's castle?
Both hands of both of you are highly worthy!
My hand has done nothing; let it be used
to save my two nephews from their death;
then I will have saved it for a worthy cause.

AARON.
Nay, come, agree whose hand shall go along,
For fear they die before their pardon come.

Come on now, agree whose hand will go along,
in case they are executed before the pardon comes.

MARCUS.
My hand shall go.

My hand shall go.

LUCIUS.
By heaven, it shall not go!

By heaven, it shall not!

TITUS.
Sirs, strive no more; such with'red herbs as these
Are meet for plucking up, and therefore mine.

Sirs, no more argument; withered flowers like these
are ready to be plucked, so mine will go.

LUCIUS.
Sweet father, if I shall be thought thy son,
Let me redeem my brothers both from death.

Sweet father, if I am worthy of being your son,
let me save my brothers from death.

MARCUS.
And for our father's sake and mother's care,

Now let me show a brother's love to thee.

And to repay our father and mother who looked after
you,
let me show a brother's love to you.

TITUS.
Agree between you; I will spare my hand.

You agree between you who shall give a hand, I'll
keep mine.

LUCIUS.
Then I'll go fetch an axe.

I'll go and get an axe

MARCUS.
But I will use the axe.
Exeunt LUCIUS and MARCUS

But I will use it.

TITUS.
Come hither, Aaron, I'll deceive them both;
Lend me thy hand, and I will give thee mine.

Come here, Aaron, I'll deceive both of them;
give me your hand, and I'll give you mine.

AARON.
[Aside] If that be call'd deceit, I will be honest,
And never whilst I live deceive men so;
But I'll deceive you in another sort,
And that you'll say ere half an hour pass.
 [He cuts off TITUS' hand]
Re-enter LUCIUS and MARCUS

If that's deceit, I'll be honest,
and never in my life deceive men like this;
but I'm deceiving you in a different way,
as you'll know before half an hour has passed.

TITUS.
Now stay your strife. What shall be is dispatch'd.
Good Aaron, give his Majesty my hand;
Tell him it was a hand that warded him
From thousand dangers; bid him bury it.
More hath it merited- that let it have.
As for my sons, say I account of them
As jewels purchas'd at an easy price;
And yet dear too, because I bought mine own.

Now stop your arguments. The deed is done.
Good Aaron, give his majesty my hand;
tell him it was the hand which protected him
from a thousand dangers; tell him to give it a burial.
It deserved more - at least give it that.
As for my sons, say that I think they are jewels
that I have bought for a bargain price;
and yet they were expensive too, for I have bought
my own goods.

AARON.
I go, Andronicus; and for thy hand

Look by and by to have thy sons with thee.
[Aside] Their heads I mean. O, how this villainy
Doth fat me with the very thoughts of it!
Let fools do good, and fair men call for grace:
Aaron will have his soul black like his face.
Exit

I'm going, Andronicus; and in exchange for your hand
expect to have your sons with you shortly.
[Aside] Their heads I mean. Oh, how this villainy
delights me even to think of it!
Let fools do good, and kind men call for kindness:
Aaron enjoys having a soul as black as his face.

TITUS.
O, here I lift this one hand up to heaven,
And bow this feeble ruin to the earth;
If any power pities wretched tears,
To that I call! [To LAVINIA] What, would'st thou
 kneel with me?
Do, then, dear heart; for heaven shall hear our
prayers,
Or with our sighs we'll breathe the welkin dim
And stain the sun with fog, as sometime clouds

Oh, I lift this one hand up to heaven,
and bow this feeble ruin down to earth.
if there is any power which pities wretched tears,
I call on it! What, do you want to kneel with me?

Then do, sweetheart; for heaven will hear our
prayers,
or we'll make the skies do more with our sighs
and cover the sun with fog, as sometimes clouds

When they do **hug him** in their melting bosoms.

do when they cover him over.

MARCUS.
O brother, speak with possibility,
And do not **break** into these deep extremes.

Oh brother, speak realistically,
and do not plumb such depths.

TITUS. Is not **my** sorrow deep, having no bottom?
Then be my **passions** bottomless with them.

Isn't my sorrow deep, being bottomless?
Then let my emotions be bottomless with them.

MARCUS.
But yet let reason govern thy lament.

But let your sadness be reasonable.

TITUS.
If there were **reason** for these miseries,
Then into limits could I bind my woes.
When heaven **doth weep**, doth not the earth o'erflow?
If the winds **rage**, doth not the sea wax mad,
Threat'ning the **welkin** with his big-swol'n face?
And wilt thou **have** a reason for this coil?
I am the sea; **hark** how her sighs do blow.
She is the weeping welkin, I the earth;
Then must my **sea** be moved with her sighs;
Then must my **earth** with her continual tears
Become a deluge, overflow'd and drown'd;
For why my bowels cannot hide her woes,
But like a drunkard must I vomit them.
Then give me leave; for losers will have leave
To ease their **stomachs** with their bitter tongues.
Enter a MESSENGER, with two heads and a hand

If there was a reason for these miseries,
then I could keep my sorrows within limits.
When heaven weeps, doesn't the Earth flood?

If the winds roar, doesn't the sea rage,
threatening the sky with his swollen waters?
And do you ask for a reason for this turmoil?
I am the sea; hear how her sighs below.
She is the weeping sky, I am the Earth.
So my sea must be moved with her sighs,
my earth must be flooded over with her
continual tears,
because my depths cannot soak up her sorrows,
but I must throw them up like a drunkard.
So give me permission, for losers must be allowed
to let their passions out with their bitter tongues.

MESSENGER.
Worthy Andronicus, ill art thou repaid
For that good **hand** thou sent'st the Emperor.
Here are the **heads** of thy two noble sons;
And here's thy **hand**, in scorn to thee sent back-
Thy grief their **sports**, thy resolution mock'd,
That woe is me to think upon thy woes,
More than remembrance of my father's death.

Good Andronicus, you have been poorly repaid
for the good hand that you sent to the Emperor.
Here are the heads of your two noble sons;
and here's your hand, sent back to you in contempt—
your sorrow is their game, your strength is mocked,
so that I am sorrowful to think of your sorrow,
it makes me sadder than thinking of the death of my
father.

Exit

MARCUS.
Now let hot **Aetna** cool in Sicily,
And be my heart an ever-burning hell!
These miseries **are** more than may be borne.
To weep with **them** that weep doth ease some deal,

Now let hot Etna in Sicily cool down,
and let my heart be an eternally burning hell!
These miseries are too great to be endured.
To weep with those who are weeping gives some

54

But sorrow flouted at is double death.

relief,
but sorrow mocked makes the death happen over
again.

LUCIUS.
Ah, that this sight should make so deep a wound,
And yet detested life not shrink thereat!
That ever death should let life bear his name,
Where life hath no more interest but to breathe!

Alas, that this sight should be so painful,
and yet not kill one!
That one should have to endure a living death,
when the only thing that shows we are alive is that
we're still breathing.

[LAVINIA kisses TITUS]

MARCUS.
Alas, poor heart, that kiss is comfortless
As frozen water to a starved snake.

Alas, poor sweetheart, that kiss has as little comfort
as frozen water gives to a freezing snake.

TITUS.
When will this fearful slumber have an end?

When will this terrible nightmare end?

MARCUS.
Now farewell, flatt'ry; die, Andronicus.
Thou dost not slumber: see thy two sons' heads,

Thy warlike hand, thy mangled daughter here;
Thy other banish'd son with this dear sight
Struck pale and bloodless; and thy brother, I,
Even like a stony image, cold and numb.
Ah! now no more will I control thy griefs.
Rent off thy silver hair, thy other hand
Gnawing with thy teeth; and be this dismal sight
The closing up of our most wretched eyes.
Now is a time to storm; why art thou still?

Enough delusion; die, Andronicus.
you are not sleeping: look at the heads of your two
sons,
your warrior's hand, your mangled daughter there;
your other exiled son struck pale and terrified
with this awful sight, and me, your brother,
cold and numb like a statue.
I will no longer tell you to hold your grief in check:
tear out your silver hair, chew off your
other hand with your teeth, and let this terrible sight
close up our wretched eyes.
Now is the time to rage. Why are you calm?

TITUS.
Ha, ha, ha!

Hah, hah, hah!

MARCUS.
Why dost thou laugh? It fits not with this hour.

Why are you laughing? It doesn't suit this time.

TITUS.
Why, I have not another tear to shed;
Besides, this sorrow is an enemy,
And would usurp upon my wat'ry eyes
And make them blind with tributary tears.
Then which way shall I find Revenge's cave?

For these two heads do seem to speak to me,
And threat me I shall never come to bliss

Why? I have no more tears to shed.
Besides, sorrow is an enemy
that wants to overthrow my watery eyes
and blind them with my tears.
Then how would I find my way to the home of
revenge?
These two heads seem to speak to me
and tell me that I shall never find happiness

Till all these mischiefs be return'd again
Even in their throats that have committed them.
Come, let me see what task I have to do.
You heavy people, circle me about,
That I may turn me to each one of you
And swear unto my soul to right your wrongs.
The vow is made. Come, brother, take a head,
And in this hand the other will I bear.
And, Lavinia, thou shalt be employ'd in this;
Bear thou my hand, sweet wench, between thy teeth.
As for thee, boy, go, get thee from my sight;
Thou art an exile, and thou must not stay.
Hie to the Goths and raise an army there;
And if ye love me, as I think you do,
Let's kiss and part, for we have much to do.
  Exeunt all but Lucius

LUCIUS.
Farewell, Andronicus, my noble father,
The woefull'st man that ever liv'd in Rome.
Farewell, proud Rome; till Lucius come again,
He leaves his pledges dearer than his life.
Farewell, Lavinia, my noble sister;
O, would thou wert as thou tofore hast been!
But now nor Lucius nor Lavinia lives
But in oblivion and hateful griefs.
If Lucius live, he will requite your wrongs

And make proud Saturnine and his emperess
Beg at the gates like Tarquin and his queen.
Now will I to the Goths, and raise a pow'r
To be reveng'd on Rome and Saturnine.
  Exit

*until these evil deeds are thrown back
in the faces of those who did them.
Come, let me see what has to be done.
You sad people, gather around me,
so that I can turn to each one of you
and swear to myself that I will revenge your wrongs.
We have made a vow. Come, brother, take a head,
and I will carry the other in this hand.
And, Lavinia, you shall have a job:
carry my hand, sweet girl, between your teeth.
As for you, boy, take yourself out of my sight:
you are an exile and you must not stay here;
go to the Goths and raise an army there,
and if you love me, as I think you do,
let's kiss and part, for we have much to do.*

*Farewell, Andronicus, my noble father,
the saddest man that ever lived in Rome.
Farewell, proud Rome; until Lucius comes again,
he leaves guarantees dearer than his life.
Farewell, Lavinia, my noble sister;
oh, if only you were the same as you were before!
But now neither Lucius nor Lavinia lives
except in their oblivion and hateful griefs.
If I live I will revenge the wrongs which have been
done to you
and makeproud Saturnine and his Empress
beg at the gates like Tarquin and his queen.
Now I will go to the Goths and raise an army,
to take revenge on Rome and Saturnine.*

SCENE II. Rome. TITUS' house

A banquet.

Enter TITUS, MARCUS, LAVINIA, and the boy YOUNG LUCIUS

TITUS.
So so, now sit; and look you eat no more
Than will preserve just so much strength in us
As will revenge these bitter woes of ours.
Marcus, unknit that sorrow-wreathen knot;
Thy niece and I, poor creatures, want our hands,

And cannot passionate our tenfold grief
With folded arms. This poor right hand of mine
Is left to tyrannize upon my breast;
Who, when my heart, all mad with misery,
Beats in this hollow prison of my flesh,
Then thus I thump it down.
[To LAVINIA] Thou map of woe, that thus dost talk
 in signs!
When thy poor heart beats with outrageous beating,
Thou canst not strike it thus to make it still.
Wound it with sighing, girl, kill it with groans;

Or get some little knife between thy teeth
And just against thy heart make thou a hole,
That all the tears that thy poor eyes let fall
May run into that sink and, soaking in,
Drown the lamenting fool in sea-salt tears.

MARCUS.
Fie, brother, fie! Teach her not thus to lay
Such violent hands upon her tender life.

TITUS.
How now! Has sorrow made thee dote already?

Why, Marcus, no man should be mad but I.

What violent hands can she lay on her life?
Ah, wherefore dost thou urge the name of hands?
To bid Aeneas tell the tale twice o'er
How Troy was burnt and he made miserable?

O, handle not the theme, to talk of hands,
Lest we remember still that we have none.

*So, now sit down; and make sure you eat just enough
to keep us just strong enough
to take revenge for our bitter sorrows.
Marcus, don't hug yourself in sorrow;
your niece and I, poor creatures, are missing our
hands,
and cannot express our ten times worse sorrows
by folding our arms. This poor right hand of mine
is left to thump my breast;
when my heart is mad with misery
and thumps inside my body's prison
then I thump it down like this.
You sorrowful figure, that has to talk in sign
language!
When your poor heart thumps with sorrow,
you can't strike it like this to calm it.
Wound it with your sighs, girl, kill it with your
groans;
or take a little knife between your teeth
and make a hole next to your heart,
so that all the tears that fall from your poor eyes
run down to that hole and sinking in
drown your sorrowing heart with salty tears.*

*Stop it, brother! Don't encourage her to
do such violent deeds.*

*What's this? Has sorrow made you feeble minded
already?
Why, Marcus, no man has more right to be mad than
I.
What violence can her hands do to her?
And why do you have to mention hands?
Would you make Aeneas tell the story twice
of how Troy was burned and he was made
miserable?
Don't use the motif of hands in your talk,
to remind us that we have none.*

Fie, fie, how franticly I square my talk,
As if we should forget we had no hands,
If Marcus did not name the word of hands!
Come, let's fall to; and, gentle girl, eat this:
Here is no drink. Hark, Marcus, what she says-

I can interpret all her martyr'd signs;
She says she drinks no other drink but tears,
Brew'd with her sorrow, mesh'd upon her cheeks.

Speechless complainer, I will learn thy thought;
In thy dumb action will I be as perfect
As begging hermits in their holy prayers.
Thou shalt not sigh, nor hold thy stumps to heaven,

Nor wink, nor nod, nor kneel, nor make a sign,
But I of these will wrest an alphabet,
And by still practice learn to know thy meaning.

BOY.
Good grandsire, leave these bitter deep laments;

Make my aunt merry with some pleasing tale.

MARCUS.
Alas, the tender boy, in passion mov'd,
Doth weep to see his grandsire's heaviness.

TITUS.
Peace, tender sapling; thou art made of tears,
And tears will quickly melt thy life away.
[MARCUS strikes the dish with a knife]
What dost thou strike at, Marcus, with thy knife?

MARCUS.
At that that I have kill'd, my lord- a fly.

TITUS.
Out on thee, murderer, thou kill'st my heart!
Mine eyes are cloy'd with view of tyranny;
A deed of death done on the innocent
Becomes not Titus' brother. Get thee gone;
I see thou art not for my company.

MARCUS.
Alas, my lord, I have but kill'd a fly.

TITUS.

Oh, how stupidly I talk,
as if we should forget that we have no hands
if Marcus didn't use the word hands!
Come, let's eat; and eat this, sweet girl:
there's no drink here. Listen to what she says,
Marcus -
I can interpret all her tortured signs;
she says she drinks no other fluid than her tears,
brewed in her sorrow, mashed* on her cheeks.
[*part of brewing]
Speechless speaker, I will learn what you think;
I will get to know your dumb signs as well
as begging hermits know their holy prayers.
You shall not sigh, nor hold your stumps up to
heaven,
nor wink, nor nod, nor kneel, nor make a sign,
without me turning them into an alphabet,
and by careful study I shall learn what you mean.

Good grandfather, leave these sorrowful speeches
alone;
cheer my aunt up with a merry story.

Alas, the sensitive boy, moved by emotion,
weeps to see his grandfather so sad.

Be calm, little one; you are full of tears,
and tears will quickly melt away your life.

What are you striking at, Marcus, with your knife?

At the thing I have killed, my lord - a fly.

Get out murderer, you've stabbed at my heart!
My eyes are choked with seeing so much tyranny;
killing the innocent is not a fitting
deed for Titus' brother. Get out;
I see you are not fit for my company.

But, my lord, I've only killed a fly.

'But!' How if that fly had a father and mother?
How would he hang his slender gilded wings
And buzz lamenting doings in the air!
Poor harmless fly,
That with his pretty buzzing melody
Came here to make us merry! And thou hast kill'd him.

MARCUS.
Pardon me, sir; it was a black ill-favour'd fly,
Like to the Empress' Moor; therefore I kill'd him.

TITUS.
O, O, O!
Then pardon me for reprehending thee,
For thou hast done a charitable deed.
Give me thy knife, I will insult on him,
Flattering myself as if it were the Moor
Come hither purposely to poison me.
There's for thyself, and that's for Tamora.
Ah, sirrah!
Yet, I think, we are not brought so low
But that between us we can kill a fly
That comes in likeness of a coal-black Moor.

MARCUS.
Alas, poor man! grief has so wrought on him,
He takes false shadows for true substances.

TITUS.
Come, take away. Lavinia, go with me;
I'll to thy closet, and go read with thee
Sad stories chanced in the times of old.
Come, boy, and go with me; thy sight is young,
And thou shalt read when mine begin to dazzle.

Exeunt

'Only!'What if that fly had a mother and a father?
How his slender shining wings would droop
and buzz sad laments in the air!
Poor harmless fly,
that with his pretty buzzing song
came here to cheer us up!And you have killed him.

Excuse me sir; it was a black ugly fly,
like the Empress' Moor; and so I killed him.

Oh-ho!
Then excuse me for telling you off,
for you have done a good deed.
Give me your knife, I will attack him,
pretending it is the Moor,
come here deliberately to poison me.
That one's for you, and that one for Tamora.
Ah, sir!
I see we have not been brought down so low
that we can't kill a fly between us
which looks like a coal-black Moor.

Alas, poor man!Grief has so turned his mind,
that he mistakes phantoms for reality.

Come, clear the table.Lavinia, come with me;
I'll come to your room, and read with you
sad stories from the olden days.
Come, boy, come with me; your eyes are young,
and you shall read when my old eyes start to fade.

ACT IV

SCENE I. Rome. TITUS' garden

Enter YOUNG LUCIUS and LAVINIA running after him, and the boy flies from her with his books under his arm.

Enter TITUS and MARCUS

BOY.
Help, grandsire, help! my aunt Lavinia
Follows me everywhere, I know not why.
Good uncle Marcus, see how swift she comes!
Alas, sweet aunt, I know not what you mean.

Help, grandfather, help! My aunt Lavinia follows me everywhere, I don't know why. Good uncle Marcus, look how she rushes at me! Alas, sweet aunt, I can't understand you.

MARCUS.
Stand by me, Lucius; do not fear thine aunt.

Stand next to me, Lucius; don't be frightened of your aunt.

TITUS.
She loves thee, boy, too well to do thee harm.

She loves you very much, boy, too much to harm you.

BOY.
Ay, when my father was in Rome she did.

Yes, she did when my father was in Rome.

MARCUS.
What means my niece Lavinia by these signs?

What does my niece Lavinia mean by these signs?

TITUS.
Fear her not, Lucius; somewhat doth she mean.

Don't be frightened of her, Lucius; she does mean something.

See, Lucius, see how much she makes of thee.
Somewhither would she have thee go with her.
Ah, boy, Cornelia never with more care
Read to her sons than she hath read to thee
Sweet poetry and Tully's Orator.

See, Lucius, what a fuss she makes of you. She wants you to go somewhere with her. Ah, boy, Cornelia never took more trouble to read to her sons than she has, reading you sweet poetry and Cicero on rhetoric.

MARCUS.
Canst thou not guess wherefore she plies thee thus?

Can't you guess why she is so attentive to you?

BOY.
My lord, I know not, I, nor can I guess,
Unless some fit or frenzy do possess her;
For I have heard my grandsire say full oft
Extremity of griefs would make men mad;
And I have read that Hecuba of Troy
Ran mad for sorrow. That made me to fear;
Although, my lord, I know my noble aunt

My lord, I don't know, nor can I guess, unless she's overcome with some fit or madness; for I have often heard my grandfather say that great grief could drive men mad; and I have read that Hecuba of Troy went mad through sorrow. That made me worry; although, my lord, I know my noble aunt

Loves me as dear as e'er my mother did,
And would not, but in fury, fright my youth;

Which made me down to throw my books, and fly-

Causeless, perhaps. But pardon me, sweet aunt;

And, madam, if my uncle Marcus go,
I will most willingly attend your ladyship.

MARCUS.
Lucius, I will. [LAVINIA turns over with her stumps the books which Lucius has let fall]

TITUS.
How now, Lavinia! Marcus, what means this?
Some book there is that she desires to see.
Which is it, girl, of these?- Open them, boy.-
But thou art deeper read and better skill'd;
Come and take choice of all my library,
And so beguile thy sorrow, till the heavens
Reveal the damn'd contriver of this deed.
Why lifts she up her arms in sequence thus?

MARCUS.
I think she means that there were more than one
Confederate in the fact; ay, more there was,
Or else to heaven she heaves them for revenge.

TITUS.
Lucius, what book is that she tosseth so?

BOY.
Grandsire, 'tis Ovid's Metamorphoses;
My mother gave it me.

MARCUS.
For love of her that's gone,
Perhaps she cull'd it from among the rest.

TITUS.
Soft! So busily she turns the leaves! Help her.

What would she find? Lavinia, shall I read?
This is the tragic tale of Philomel
And treats of Tereus' treason and his rape;
And rape, I fear, was root of thy annoy.

loves me as dearly as my mother ever did,
and would not want to scare me unless she was in a rage;
that was what made me throw down my books and run-
there was no reason to, perhaps. But forgive me, sweet aunt;
and, madam, if my uncle Marcius is going,
I will be very happy to wait on your ladyship.

Lucius, that's what I want.

What's this, Lavinia? Marcus, what does this mean?
She wants to see in one of these books.
Which of these is it, girl? - Open them, boy -
But you are better read and more intelligent;
come and take your pick from my whole library,
and so ease your pain, until the heavens
show us who did this to you.
Why does she wave her arms like this?

I think she means there was more than one
person who did this; yes, more than one.
Unless she's waving her arms to heaven for revenge.

Lucius, what's that book she's throwing around?

Grandfather, it's Ovid's Metamorphoses;
my mother gave it to me.

Perhaps she's singled it out from the rest
out of love for the one who's departed.

Hush! See how eagerly she's turning the pages! Help her.
What is she looking for? Lavinia, shall I read?
This is the tragic tale of Philomel,
which talks of Tereus' treason and his rape of her;
and rape, I fear, is at the heart of your anguish.

MARCUS.
See, brother, see! Note how she quotes the leaves.

Look brother, look! See how she's pointing out passages.

TITUS.
Lavinia, wert thou thus surpris'd, sweet girl,
Ravish'd and wrong'd as Philomela was,
Forc'd in the ruthless, vast, and gloomy woods?
See, see!
Ay, such a place there is where we did hunt-
O, had we never, never hunted there!-
Pattern'd by that the poet here describes,
By nature made for murders and for rapes.

*Lavinia, were you ambushed like this, dear girl,
raped and harmed as Philomela was,
compelled in the pitiless, vast and gloomy woods?
Look, look!
Yes, we hunted in a place like this -
Oh, I wish we'd never ever hunted there! -
a setting like the poet describes here,
created by nature for murder and rape.*

MARCUS.
O, why should nature build so foul a den,
Unless the gods delight in tragedies?

*Oh, why should nature build such a foul den,
unless the gods enjoy tragedies?*

TITUS.
Give signs, sweet girl, for here are none but friends,
What Roman lord it was durst do the deed.
Or slunk not Saturnine, as Tarquin erst,

That left the camp to sin in Lucrece' bed?

*Give signs, sweet girl, you're amongst your friends.
What Roman lord was it who dared to do the deed.
Was it Saturnine who crept up on you, like Tarquin before him,
who left the camp to sin in Lucrece's bed?*

MARCUS.
Sit down, sweet niece; brother, sit down by me.
Apollo, Pallas, Jove, or Mercury,
Inspire me, that I may this treason find!
My lord, look here! Look here, Lavinia!
[He writes his name with his
staff, and guides it with feet and mouth]
This sandy plot is plain; guide, if thou canst,

This after me. I have writ my name
Without the help of any hand at all.
Curs'd be that heart that forc'd us to this shift!
Write thou, good niece, and here display at last
What God will have discovered for revenge.
Heaven guide thy pen to print thy sorrows plain,

That we may know the traitors and the truth!
[She takes the staff in her mouth
and guides it with stumps, and writes]
O, do ye read, my lord, what she hath writ?

*Sit down, sweet niece; brother, sit down by me.
Apollo, Pallas, Jove or Mercury,
Guide me to reveal this treason!
My lord, look here! Look here, Lavinia!*

*This sandy ground is smooth; guide this stick, if you can,
like I have. I have written my name
without using my hands at all.
Damn the person who forced us to these measures!
Write, good niece, and show us at last
whom God wants us to take revenge on.
May heaven guide your pen to make your sad story clear,
So we can know the traitors and the truth!*

Oh my lord, do you see what she has written?

TITUS.

'Stuprum- Chiron- Demetrius.'

'Rape - Chiron - Demetrius.'

MARCUS. What, what! the lustful sons of Tamora
Performers of this heinous bloody deed?

What, what! The lustful sons of Tamora
were the ones who did this horrible bloody deed?

TITUS.
Magni Dominator poli,
Tam lentus audis scelera? tam lentus vides?

Ruler of the great heavens,
are you so slow to hear such great crimes? So slow
to see?

MARCUS.
O, calm thee, gentle lord! although I know
There is enough written upon this earth
To stir a mutiny in the mildest thoughts,
And arm the minds of infants to exclaims.
My lord, kneel down with me; Lavinia, kneel;
And kneel, sweet boy, the Roman Hector's hope;

Calm yourself, great lord! Although I know
there is enough written here on the earth
to cause outrage in the most gentle mind,
and start the minds of infants raging.
My lord, kneel down with me; Lavinia, kneel;
and kneel, sweet boy, whom we expect to be a
Roman Hector;

And swear with me- as, with the woeful fere
And father of that chaste dishonoured dame,
Lord Junius Brutus sware for Lucrece' rape-
That we will prosecute, by good advice,
Mortal revenge upon these traitorous Goths,
And see their blood or die with this reproach.

and swear with me - as, with his sorrowing wife,
and the father of that chaste dishonest lady,
Lord Junius Brutus swore about the rape of Lucrece -
that we will, with a good plan, take
fatal revenge on these traitorous Goths,
and see their blood or die ashamed.

TITUS.
'Tis sure enough, an you knew how;
But if you hunt these bear-whelps, then beware:
The dam will wake; and if she wind ye once,
She's with the lion deeply still in league,
And lulls him whilst she playeth on her back,
And when he sleeps will she do what she list.
You are a young huntsman, Marcus; let alone;

It's certain enough, if you find a way;
but if you hunt these bear cubs, beware:
the mother will wake, and if she scents you once,
she's still closely allied to the lion,
and she calms him by playing on her back,
and when he sleeps she does whatever she wants.
You are an inexperienced hunter, Marcus; put it to
one side;

And come, I will go get a leaf of brass,
And with a gad of steel will write these words,
And lay it by. The angry northern wind
Will blow these sands like Sibyl's leaves abroad,

look, I will get a sheet of brass,
and with a steel pen I will write these words on it
and we'll store it up. The angry north wind
will blow these sands around like the papers of the
Sybil,

And where's our lesson, then? Boy, what say you?

and where will our words be then? Boy, what do you
say?

BOY.
I say, my lord, that if I were a man
Their mother's bedchamber should not be safe
For these base bondmen to the yoke of Rome.

I say, my lord, that if I were a man
their mother's bedroom would be no safe refuge
for these slaves of Rome.

MARCUS.

Ay, that's my boy! Thy father hath full oft
For his ungrateful country done the like.

*Yes, that's my boy! Your father has often
done the same for his ungrateful country.*

BOY.
And, uncle, so will I, an if I live.

And so will I, uncle, if I live.

TITUS.
Come, go with me into mine armoury.
Lucius, I'll fit thee; and withal my boy
Shall carry from me to the Empress' sons
Presents that I intend to send them both.
Come, come; thou'lt do my message, wilt thou not?

*Come with me into my armoury.
Lucius, I'll kit you out; and soon my boy
shall take the Empress' sons
presents from me for the both of them.
Come along; you'll run my errand, won't you?*

BOY.
Ay, with my dagger in their bosoms, grandsire.

Yes, with my dagger in their hearts, grandfather.

TITUS.
No, boy, not so; I'll teach thee another course.
Lavinia, come. Marcus, look to my house.
Lucius and I'll go brave it at the court;
Ay, marry, will we, sir! and we'll be waited on.
    Exeunt TITUS, LAVINIA, and YOUNG LUCIUS

*No boy, not like that; I'll teach you a different way.
Come, Lavinia. Marcus, guard my house.
Lucius and I shall go and put on a show at the court,
we shall sir! And they'll pay attention to us.*

MARCUS.
O heavens, can you hear a good man groan
And not relent, or not compassion him?
Marcus, attend him in his ecstasy,
That hath more scars of sorrow in his heart
Than foemen's marks upon his batt'red shield,
But yet so just that he will not revenge.
Revenge the heavens for old Andronicus!
Exit

*Oh heavens, can you hear a good man groan
and not relent or feel sorry for him?
Marcus, go with him in his madness,
he has more scars of sorrow in his heart
than he has enemies' marks on his battered shield,
and yet he is so just that he won't take revenge.
Heavens, take revenge for old Andronicus!*

SCENE II. Rome. The palace

Enter AARON, DEMETRIUS and CHIRON, at one door; and at the other door, YOUNG LUCIUS and another with a bundle of weapons, and verses writ upon them

CHIRON.
Demetrius, here's the son of Lucius;
He hath some message to deliver us.

Demetrius, here's the son of Lucius;
he has some message to give us.

AARON.
Ay, some mad message from his mad grandfather.

Yes, some mad message from his mad grandfather.

BOY.
My lords, with all the humbleness I may,
I greet your honours from Andronicus-
[Aside] And pray the Roman gods confound you both!

My lords, with all the humility I have,
I bring your honours greetings from Andronicus-
[Aside] and I pray that the Roman gods damn you both.

DEMETRIUS.
Gramercy, lovely Lucius. What's the news?

We thank you, lovely Lucius. What's your news?

BOY.
[Aside] That you are both decipher'd, that's the news,
For villains mark'd with rape.- May it please you,
My grandsire, well advis'd, hath sent by me
The goodliest weapons of his armoury
To gratify your honourable youth,
The hope of Rome; for so he bid me say;
And so I do, and with his gifts present
Your lordships, that, whenever you have need,
You may be armed and appointed well.
And so I leave you both- [Aside] like bloody villains.
 Exeunt YOUNG LUCIUS and attendant

[Aside] That you have both been found out,
that's the news,
as villainous rapists. - May it please you,
my grandfather, in his right mind, has sent me with
the best weapons in his armoury
to please you noble youths,
the hope of Rome; that's what he told me to say;
and so I do, and I present your lordships
with his gifts, so that whenever you need to be
you may be well armed and dressed.
And so I leave you both - [Aside] like bloody villains.

DEMETRIUS.
What's here? A scroll, and written round about.
Let's see:
[Reads] 'Integer vitae, scelerisque purus,
Non eget Mauri iaculis, nec arcu.'

What's this? A scroll, with writing round it. Let's see:

"The man of upright life and free from crime
has no need of the slings and bows of the Moor."

CHIRON.
O, 'tis a verse in Horace, I know it well;

Oh, it's a verse from Horace, I know it well;

I read it in the grammar long ago.

AARON.
Ay, just- a verse in Horace. Right, you have it.

[Aside] Now, what a thing it is to be an ass!
Here's no sound jest! The old man hath found their guilt,
And sends them weapons wrapp'd about with lines
That wound, beyond their feeling, to the quick.

But were our witty Empress well afoot,
She would applaud Andronicus' conceit.
But let her rest in her unrest awhile-
And now, young lords, was't not a happy star
Led us to Rome, strangers, and more than so,

Captives, to be advanced to this height?
It did me good before the palace gate
To brave the Tribune in his brother's hearing.

DEMETRIUS.
But me more good to see so great a lord
Basely insinuate and send us gifts.

AARON.
Had he not reason, Lord Demetrius?
Did you not use his daughter very friendly?

DEMETRIUS.
I would we had a thousand Roman dames
At such a bay, by turn to serve our lust.

CHIRON.
A charitable wish and full of love.

AARON.
Here lacks but your mother for to say amen.

CHIRON.
And that would she for twenty thousand more.

DEMETRIUS.
Come, let us go and pray to all the gods
For our beloved mother in her pains.

I read it in a grammar long ago.

Yes, that's right - a verse in Horace. That's right, you've got it.

*[Aside] What a thing it is to be so stupid!
Here's a good joke! The old man has discovered their guilt,
and sends them weapons wrapped round with lines
that wound them, though they can't see it, to the core.
If our clever Empress was up and about
she would applaud Andronicus' joke.
But let her rest in her discomfort for a while -
And now, young lords, wasn't it a lucky star
that brought us to Rome as foreigners, and more than that,
prisoners, and now raises us so high?
it did me good at the gates of the palace
to face down the Tribune in his brother's presence.*

*But it did me more good to see such a great lord
grovel so low and send us gifts.*

*Didn't he have reason to, Lord Demetrius?
Weren't you very friendly to his daughter?*

*I wish we had a thousand Roman ladies
cornered like that, to serve our lusts in turn.*

A kind wish and full of love.

All that's missing is for your mother to agree.

And she would agree to our having twenty thousand more.

*Come, let us go and pray to all the gods,
for our beloved mother in her labour.*

AARON.
[Aside] Pray to the devils; the gods have given us
over.
[Trumpets sound]

Pray to the devils; the gods have given up on us.

DEMETRIUS.
Why do the Emperor's trumpets flourish thus?

Why do the Emperor's trumpets give such a blast?

CHIRON.
Belike, for joy the Emperor hath a son.

*I expect it's from joy because the Emperor has had a
son.*

DEMETRIUS.
Soft! who comes here?
Enter NURSE, with a blackamoor CHILD

Wait!Who's this?

NURSE.
Good morrow, lords.
O, tell me, did you see Aaron the Moor?

*Good day, lords.
Tell me, have you seen Aaron the Moor?*

AARON.
Well, more or less, or ne'er a whit at all,
Here Aaron is; and what with Aaron now?

*Well, I should think we have,
here's Aaron; and what do you what with him?*

NURSE.
O gentle Aaron, we are all undone!
Now help, or woe betide thee evermore!

*Oh sweet Aaron, we are all overthrown!
Now help, or you're lost forever!*

AARON.
Why, what a caterwauling dost thou keep!
What dost thou wrap and fumble in thy arms?

*What a racket you're making!
What's that you've got wrapped up in your arms?*

NURSE.
O, that which I would hide from heaven's eye:

*Something which I would like to hide from the sight
of heaven:*

Our Empress' shame and stately Rome's disgrace!

*the shame of our Empress and the disgrace of great
Rome!*

She is delivered, lord; she is delivered.

She has had it, my lord.

AARON.
To whom?

Had who?

NURSE.
I mean she is brought a-bed.

I mean she's been confined to her bed..

AARON.
Well, God give her good rest! What hath he sent
her?

*Well, may God give her a good rest!What has he
sent her?*

NURSE.
A devil.

A devil.

AARON.
Why, then she is the devil's dam;
A joyful issue.

Why then, she's the devil's mother;
a happy result.

NURSE.
A joyless, dismal, black, and sorrowful issue!
Here is the babe, as loathsome as a toad
Amongst the fair-fac'd breeders of our clime;
The Empress sends it thee, thy stamp, thy seal,

And bids thee christen it with thy dagger's point.

A joyless, dismal, black and sorrowful result!
Here is the baby, as horrid as a toad
amongst the fair-faced parents of our region;
the Empress sends it to you, with your image
stamped on it,
and tells you to christen it with the point of your
dagger.

AARON.
Zounds, ye whore! Is black so base a hue?

Sweet blowse, you are a beauteous blossom sure.

Good heavens, you whore! Is black such a bad
colour?
Sweet ruddiness, you are a lovely lad.

DEMETRIUS.
Villain, what hast thou done?

Villain, what have you done?

AARON.
That which thou canst not undo.

Something you can't undo.

CHIRON.
Thou hast undone our mother.

You have undone our mother.

AARON.
Villain, I have done thy mother.

Villain, I have done your mother.

DEMETRIUS.
And therein, hellish dog, thou hast undone her.

Woe to her chance, and damn'd her loathed choice!

Accurs'd the offspring of so foul a fiend!

And by doing so, you hellish dog, you have undone
her.
What terrible luck, and what a horrible choice she
made!
Curses on the child of such a devil!

CHIRON.
It shall not live.

It shall not live.

AARON.
It shall not die.

It shall not die.

NURSE.
Aaron, it must; the mother wills it so.

Aaron, it must; its mother orders it.

AARON.
What, must it, nurse? Then let no man but I
Do execution on my flesh and blood.

*It must, must it nurse? Then let nobody but me
execute my own flesh and blood.*

DEMETRIUS.
I'll broach the tadpole on my rapier's point.
Nurse, give it me; my sword shall soon dispatch it.

*I'll stick the tadpole on the point of my rapier.
Nurse, give it to me; my sword will soon dispatch it.*

AARON.
Sooner this sword shall plough thy bowels up.
[Takes the CHILD from the NURSE, and draws]
Stay, murderous villains, will you kill your brother!

This sword will rip you open before you do.

*Stop you murderous villains, will you kill your
brother!*

Now, by the burning tapers of the sky
That shone so brightly when this boy was got,
He dies upon my scimitar's sharp point
That touches this my first-born son and heir.
I tell you, younglings, not Enceladus,
With all his threat'ning band of Typhon's brood,
Nor great Alcides, nor the god of war,
Shall seize this prey out of his father's hands.
What, what, ye sanguine, shallow-hearted boys!
Ye white-lim'd walls! ye alehouse painted signs!

*Now, by the stars in the sky,
that shone so brightly when this boy was conceived,
he dies on the sharp point of my scimitar
that touches my first born son and heir.
I tell you, youngsters, not Enceladus,
with all his threatening band of giants,
Nor great Alcides, nor the god of war,
shall seize this prey from his father's hands.
What, you red faced, shallow hearted boys!
You whitewashed walls! You crudely painted
pictures!*

Coal-black is better than another hue
In that it scorns to bear another hue;
For all the water in the ocean
Can never turn the swan's black legs to white,
Although she lave them hourly in the flood.
Tell the Empress from me I am of age
To keep mine own- excuse it how she can.

*Coal black is the best colour,
because it doesn't change to another colour.
All the water in the ocean
Can never turn the swan's black legs to white,
however long she washes them in the tides.
tell the Empress that I'm old enough to look
after this child myself; she must make whatever
excuse she thinks best.*

DEMETRIUS.
Wilt thou betray thy noble mistress thus?

Will you betray your noble mistress this way?

AARON.
My mistress is my mistress: this my self,
The vigour and the picture of my youth.
This before all the world do I prefer;
This maugre all the world will I keep safe,

*My mistress is my mistress: this is myself,
a perfect copy of the strength of my childhood.
I prefer this above the whole world;
I shall keep this in the face of the whole world's
opposition,*

Or some of you shall smoke for it in Rome.

or some of you in Rome shall suffer for it.

DEMETRIUS.
By this our mother is for ever sham'd.

Our mother is eternally shamed by this.

CHIRON.
Rome will despise her for this foul escape.

Rome will despise her for this foul adventure.

NURSE.
The Emperor in his rage will doom her death.

The Emperor will sentence her to death in his rage.

CHIRON.
I blush to think upon this ignomy.

I blush to think of the shame.

AARON.
Why, there's the privilege your beauty bears:
Fie, treacherous hue, that will betray with blushing

The close enacts and counsels of thy heart!
Here's a young lad fram'd of another leer.
Look how the black slave smiles upon the father,
As who should say 'Old lad, I am thine own.'
He is your brother, lords, sensibly fed
Of that self-blood that first gave life to you;
And from your womb where you imprisoned were
He is enfranchised and come to light.
Nay, he is your brother by the surer side,
Although my seal be stamped in his face.

Why, there's the privilege of your colour:
Pah, what a treacherous colour, that exposes by blushing,
the hidden thoughts and desires of your heart!
Here's a young lad painted with a different brush.
Look how the black slave smiles at his father,
as if he's saying, "Old lad, I am your own."
He is your brother, lords, clearly nurtured
by the same blood that gave you life;
from the womb where you were imprisoned
he has been set free and come to light.
There's no way to deny he is your brother,
even if my looks are stamped on his face.

NURSE.
Aaron, what shall I say unto the Empress?

Aaron, what shall I say to the Empress?

DEMETRIUS.
Advise thee, Aaron, what is to be done,
And we will all subscribe to thy advice.
Save thou the child, so we may all be safe.

You tell us, Aaron, what should be done,
and we will all follow your advice.
Save the child, provided you can keep us all safe.

AARON.
Then sit we down and let us all consult.
My son and I will have the wind of you:
Keep there; now talk at pleasure of your safety.

So let's sit down and decide what to do.
My son and I have our eye on you:
stay there; now talk of your preservation how you wish.

[They sit]

DEMETRIUS.
How many women saw this child of his?

How many women saw this child of his?

AARON.
Why, so, brave lords! When we join in league
I am a lamb; but if you brave the Moor,
The chafed boar, the mountain lioness,
The ocean swells not so as Aaron storms.
But say, again, how many saw the child?

What's this, brave lords! If we work together
I'll be a lamb; but if you challenge the Moor,
the angry boar, the mountain lioness,
the ocean, will not rage like Aaron.
But, tell us, how many saw the child?

NURSE.
Cornelia the midwife and myself;
And no one else but the delivered Empress.

The midwife Cornelia and myself;
nobody else but the Empress who gave birth.

AARON.
The Emperess, the midwife, and yourself.
Two may keep counsel when the third's away:
Go to the Empress, tell her this I said. [He kills her]

The Empress, the midwife, and you.
Two can keep their secret when the third's not there:
go to the Empress and tell her I said this [He kills her]

Weeke weeke!
So cries a pig prepared to the spit.

Wee wee!
So the pig cries when it's spitted.

DEMETRIUS.
What mean'st thou, Aaron? Wherefore didst thou this?

What are you doing, Aaron? Why did you do this?

AARON.
O Lord, sir, 'tis a deed of policy.
Shall she live to betray this guilt of ours-
A long-tongu'd babbling gossip? No, lords, no.
And now be it known to you my full intent:
Not far, one Muliteus, my countryman-
His wife but yesternight was brought to bed;
His child is like to her, fair as you are.
Go pack with him, and give the mother gold,
And tell them both the circumstance of all,
And how by this their child shall be advanc'd,
And be received for the Emperor's heir
And substituted in the place of mine,
To calm this tempest whirling in the court;
And let the Emperor dandle him for his own.
Hark ye, lords. You see I have given her physic,
[Pointing to the NURSE]
And you must needs bestow her funeral;
The fields are near, and you are gallant grooms.
This done, see that you take no longer days,
But send the midwife presently to me.
The midwife and the nurse well made away,

Then let the ladies tattle what they please.

Oh Lord, sir, it's the strategic thing to do.
Should she live to betray our guilt -
a wagging-tongued gossip? No, lords, no.
And now I'll tell you my whole plan:
Not far from here there's my countryman Muliteus-
his wife went into labour just last night;
his child is like her, as fair as you are.
Go and plot with him, and give the mother gold,
and tell them both what's going on,
and how their child shall be advanced,
and be taken as the Emperor's heir
and put in place of my own child,
to calm this great storm in the court;
let the Emperor raise him as his own.
Listen, lords. You see I have given her medicine,

and you will have to organise her funeral;
the fields are close, and you are noble pallbearers.
When you've done that, don't delay any further,
but send the midwife to me at once.
Once the midwife and the nurse have been disposed of
let the gossips say what they please.

CHIRON.

Aaron, I see thou wilt not trust the air
With secrets.

Aaron, I see you won't let any secrets get out.

DEMETRIUS.
For this care of Tamora,
Herself and hers are highly bound to thee.
Exeunt DEMETRIUS and CHIRON, bearing off the dead NURSE

For taking such care of Tamora,
she and her family are greatly indebted to you.

AARON.
Now to the Goths, as swift as swallow flies,

Now I shall go to the Goths, as quick as the swallow flies,

There to dispose this treasure in mine arms,
And secretly to greet the Empress' friends.
Come on, you thick-lipp'd slave, I'll bear you hence;
For it is you that puts us to our shifts.
I'll make you feed on berries and on roots,
And feed on curds and whey, and suck the goat,
And cabin in a cave, and bring you up
To be a warrior and command a camp.
 Exit with the CHILD

to hide this treasure I hold in my arms,
and to secretly meet the Empress' friends.
Come on, you thick-lipped slave, I'll carry you away;
You're the one causing all this commotion.
I'll feed you on roots and berries,
curds and whey, you shall suckle from a goat,
and live in a cave, and I'll bring you up
to be a warrior and command an army.

SCENE III. Rome. A public place

Enter TITUS, bearing arrows with letters on the ends of them; with him MARCUS, YOUNG LUCIUS, and other gentlemen, PUBLIUS, SEMPRONIUS, and CAIUS, with bows

TITUS.
Come, Marcus, come; kinsmen, this is the way.
Sir boy, let me see your archery;
Look ye draw home enough, and 'tis there straight.

Terras Astrea reliquit,
Be you rememb'red, Marcus; she's gone, she's fled.
Sirs, take you to your tools. You, cousins, shall
Go sound the ocean and cast your nets;
Happily you may catch her in the sea;
Yet there's as little justice as at land.
No; Publius and Sempronius, you must do it;
'Tis you must dig with mattock and with spade,
And pierce the inmost centre of the earth;
Then, when you come to Pluto's region,
I pray you deliver him this petition.
Tell him it is for justice and for aid,
And that it comes from old Andronicus,
Shaken with sorrows in ungrateful Rome.
Ah, Rome! Well, well, I made thee miserable
What time I threw the people's suffrages
On him that thus doth tyrannize o'er me.
Go get you gone; and pray be careful all,
And leave you not a man-of-war unsearch'd.
This wicked Emperor may have shipp'd her hence;
And, kinsmen, then we may go pipe for justice.

MARCUS.
O Publius, is not this a heavy case,
To see thy noble uncle thus distract?

PUBLIUS.
Therefore, my lords, it highly us concerns
By day and night t' attend him carefully,
And feed his humour kindly as we may
Till time beget some careful remedy.

MARCUS.
Kinsmen, his sorrows are past remedy.
Join with the Goths, and with revengeful war
Take wreak on Rome for this ingratitude,

Come on Marcus, come; kinsmen, this is the way.
You boy, let me see your archery;
make sure you draw the bow far enough back and you'll hit the target.
Astrea has left the earth,
Remember that, Marcus; she's gone, she's fled.
Sirs, get your tools ready. You, cousins, will
go and throw your nets into the ocean;
with luck you might catch her in the sea;
but there's just as little justice on land.
No; Publius and Sempronius, you must do it;
you must dig with spade and fork,
and get right into the heart of the earth;
then, when you get to hell,
please give Pluto this petition.
Tell him it's asking for justice and help,
and that it comes from old Andronicus,
shaken with sorrows in ungrateful Rome.
Ah, Rome! Well, well, I made you miserable
the time I bestowed the people's votes
on the one who now tortures me.
Off you go; and please all be careful,
and don't leave a single warship unsearched.
The wicked Emperor may have shipped her out;
if that's happened, kinsmen, we can whistle for justice.

Oh Publius, isn't this awful,
to see your noble uncle so mad?

So, my lords, we must be very diligent
and be with him night and day,
and look after him as best we can
until time heals him.

Kinsmen, his grief is beyond healing.
Join the Goths and start a war of revenge
to punish Rome for this ingratitude

And vengeance on the traitor Saturnine.

and to punish the traitor Saturnine.

TITUS.
Publius, how now? How now, my masters?

Publius, what's happening? What's the story, my masters?

What, have you met with her?

What, have you met her?

PUBLIUS.
No, my good lord; but Pluto sends you word,
If you will have Revenge from hell, you shall.

No, my good lord; but Pluto sends word to you that if you want revenge from hell then you shall have it.

Marry, for Justice, she is so employ'd,
He thinks, with Jove in heaven, or somewhere else,
So that perforce you must needs stay a time.

As for Justice, he thinks that she's working with Jove in heaven, or elsewhere, So that you'll have to wait a while.

TITUS.
He doth me wrong to feed me with delays.
I'll dive into the burning lake below
And pull her out of Acheron by the heels.
Marcus, we are but shrubs, no cedars we,
No big-bon'd men fram'd of the Cyclops' size;
But metal, Marcus, steel to the very back,
Yet wrung with wrongs more than our backs can bear;
And, sith there's no justice in earth nor hell,
We will solicit heaven, and move the gods
To send down justice for to wreak our wrongs.
Come, to this gear. You are a good archer, Marcus.

It's not right of him to keep me waiting. I'll dive into the burning lake below and pull her out of Acheron by the heels. Marcus, we're just shrubs, not cedars, not big boned men shaped like the Cyclops; but we're strong, Marcus, steel through and through, though we're loaded down with more wrongs than we can carry; and, since there's no justice on earth or in hell, we call on heaven, and ask the gods to send down justice to avenge our wrongs. Come, let's look to our weaponry. You're a good archer, Marcus.

[He gives them the arrows]
'Ad Jovem' that's for you; here 'Ad Apollinem.'
'Ad Martem' that's for myself.
Here, boy, 'To Pallas'; here 'To Mercury.'
'To Saturn,' Caius- not to Saturnine:
You were as good to shoot against the wind.

[he gives them arrows] "To Jove' - that's for you; here 'to Apollo' and 'to Mars', that's for myself. Here, boy, 'to Pallas'; here 'to Mercury.' 'To Saturn', Caius - not to Saturnine: you might as well shoot into the wind as ask him for anything.

To it, boy. Marcus, loose when I bid.
Of my word, I have written to effect;
There's not a god left unsolicited.

Let's go to it, boy. Marcus, fire when I order. I have written all I mean; there's not a god I haven't called on.

MARCUS.
Kinsmen, shoot all your shafts into the court;
We will afflict the Emperor in his pride.

Kinsmen, shoot all your arrows into the court; we'll hit the Emperor in his own home.

TITUS.
Now, masters, draw. [They shoot] O, well said, Lucius!

Now, masters, draw. [they shoot]Oh, well done, Lucius!

Good boy, in Virgo's lap! Give it Pallas.

Good boy, right into Virgo! Now fire at Athene.

MARCUS.
My lord, I aim a mile beyond the moon;
Your letter is with Jupiter by this.

My lord, I aimed a mile past the moon;
your request will reach Jupiter like this.

TITUS. Ha! ha!
Publius, Publius, hast thou done?
See, see, thou hast shot off one of Taurus' horns.

Ha! Ha!
Publius, Publius, have you finished?
Look, you've shot off one of Taurus' horns.

MARCUS.
This was the sport, my lord: when Publius shot,
The Bull, being gall'd, gave Aries such a knock
That down fell both the Ram's horns in the court;
And who should find them but the Empress' villain?
She laugh'd, and told the Moor he should not choose

But give them to his master for a present.

That was the game, my lord: when Publius shot,
the Bull, being grazed, gave Aries such a knock
that both his Ram's horns fell down into the court;
and who should find them but the Empress' villain?
She laughed, and told the Moor he could do no
better
than to put the horns on the Emperor as a gift.

TITUS.
Why, there it goes! God give his lordship joy!
Enter the CLOWN, with a basket and two pigeons in it
News, news from heaven! Marcus, the post is come.
Sirrah, what tidings? Have you any letters?
Shall I have justice? What says Jupiter?

Why, there they go! May God give him happiness!

News, news from heaven! Marcus, the post has come.
Sir, what news? Have you any letters?
Shall I have justice? What does Jupiter say?

CLOWN.
Ho, the gibbet-maker? He says that he hath taken
them down
again, for the man must not be hang'd till the next
week.
TITUS.
But what says Jupiter, I ask thee?

What, you mean the gibbet maker? He says he's
taken the scaffold down,
as the man has a reprieve until next week.

But I'm asking you what does Jupiter say?

CLOWN.
Alas, sir, I know not Jupiter; I never drank with
him in all my life.

Alas, sir, I don't know Jupiter; I never drank
with him in my life.

TITUS.
Why, villain, art not thou the carrier?

Why, you villain, aren't you the porter [of
messages]?

CLOWN.
Ay, of my pigeons, sir; nothing else.

Yes, of my pigeons, sir; nothing else.

TITUS.
Why, didst thou not come from heaven?

Well, didn't you come from heaven?

CLOWN.

From heaven! Alas, sir, I never came there. God forbid I
should be so bold to press to heaven in my young days. Why, I
amgoing with my pigeons to the Tribunal Plebs, to take up a matter
of brawl betwixt my uncle and one of the Emperal's men.

From heaven!Alas, sir, I've never been there.God forbid I should be making visits to heaven when I'm still so young. I'm going with my pigeons to the plebeian court, to try and settle a matter of a brawl between my uncle and one of the emperor's men.

MARCUS.

Why, sir, that is as fit as can be to serve for your oration; and let him deliver the pigeons to the Emperor from you.

Why, sir, this is as good as anything for your speech, let him deliver the pigeons from the Emperor to you.

TITUS.

Tell me, can you deliver an oration to the Emperor with a grace?

Tell me, can you deliver a speech to the Emperor with grace?

CLOWN.

Nay, truly, sir, I could never say grace in all my life.

No, honestly, sir, I never said grace in my life.

TITUS.

Sirrah, come hither. Make no more ado,
But give your pigeons to the Emperor;
By me thou shalt have justice at his hands.
Hold, hold! Meanwhile here's money for thy charges.
Give me pen and ink. Sirrah, can you with a grace deliver up a supplication?

Sir, come here.No more joking. Just give your pigeons to the Emperor; through me he shall give you justice. Wait, wait!Here's money for your expenses. Give me a pen and ink.Sir, can you deliver a plea politely?

CLOWN.

Ay, sir.

Yes, sir.

TITUS.

Then here is a supplication for you. And when you come
to
him, at the first approach you must kneel; then kiss his foot;
then deliver up your pigeons; and then look for your reward. I'll
be at hand, sir; see you do it bravely.

Then here is a plea for you.And when you come to him, you must kneel, and then kiss his foot, then give him your pigeons, and then see what you get. I'll be standing by, sir, to see you do it well.

CLOWN.

I warrant you, sir; let me alone.

I promise I will sir, trust me for that.

TITUS.

Sirrah, hast thou a knife? Come let me see it.
Here, Marcus, fold it in the oration;
For thou must hold it like a humbx`le suppliant.
And when thou hast given it to the Emperor,
Knock at my door, and tell me what he says.

CLOWN.
God be with you, sir; I will.

TITUS.
Come, Marcus, let us go. Publius, follow me.
Exeunt

Sir, do you have a knife? Come, let me see it.
Here, Marcus, fold the speech round it;
you must hold it like a humble petitioner.
and when you have given it to the Emperor,
come to my house and tell me what he said.

God be with you sir; I shall.

Come, Marcus, let us go. Publius, follow me.

SCENE IV. Rome. Before the palace

Enter the EMPEROR, and the EMPRESS and her two sons, DEMETRIUS
and CHIRON; LORDS and others. The EMPEROR brings the arrows in his hand that
TITUS shot at him

SATURNINUS.

Why, lords, what wrongs are these! Was ever seen	*Why, lords, what crimes have been done! Was there ever*
An emperor in Rome thus overborne,	*a Roman Emperor who was so overwhelmed,*
Troubled, confronted thus; and, for the extent	*so troubled, so challenged, and treated with such*
Of egal justice, us'd in such contempt?	*contempt for handing out equal justice?*
My lords, you know, as know the mightful gods,	*My lords, you know, as the mighty gods do,*
However these disturbers of our peace	*whatever these disturbers of the peace*
Buzz in the people's ears, there nought hath pass'd	*whisper in people's ears, nothing happened*
But even with law against the wilful sons	*with the disobedient sons of old Andronicus*
Of old Andronicus. And what an if	*that wasn't within the law. And so what if*
His sorrows have so overwhelm'd his wits,	*his grief has so triumphed over his sense,*
Shall we be thus afflicted in his wreaks,	*should we suffer for his acts of revenge,*
His fits, his frenzy, and his bitterness?	*his moods, his madness and his bitterness?*
And now he writes to heaven for his redress.	*And now he calls on heaven for revenge.*
See, here's 'To Jove' and this 'To Mercury';	*Look, here it says, "To Jove" and here, "To Mercury";*
This 'To Apollo'; this 'To the God of War'-	*this says, "To Apollo"; this "To the God of War" -*
Sweet scrolls to fly about the streets of Rome!	*Nice things to have flying around the streets of Rome!*
What's this but libelling against the Senate,	*What are these but libels against the Senate,*
And blazoning our unjustice every where?	*calling us unjust everywhere?*
A goodly humour, is it not, my lords?	*A nice trick, isn't it, my lords?*
As who would say in Rome no justice were.	*He's claiming that there's no justice in Rome.*
But if I live, his feigned ecstasies	*But if I live his faked madness*
Shall be no shelter to these outrages;	*will not excuse this outrageous behaviour;*
But he and his shall know that justice lives	*he and his family shall know that justice still lives*
In Saturninus' health; whom, if she sleep,	*as long as Saturninus does; if she sleeps,*
He'll so awake as she in fury shall	*I'll stir her up into such a frenzy that she will*
Cut off the proud'st conspirator that lives.	*cut down the proudest conspirator who ever lived.*

TAMORA.

My gracious lord, my lovely Saturnine,	*My gracious lord, my lovely Saturnine,*
Lord of my life, commander of my thoughts,	*Lord of my life, commander of my thoughts,*
Calm thee, and bear the faults of Titus' age,	*calm yourself, and tolerate the faults of the old man Titus,*
Th' effects of sorrow for his valiant sons	*and his behaviour which is caused by sorrow for his sons' death,*
Whose loss hath pierc'd him deep and scarr'd his heart;	*whose loss has stabbed him right to the heart;*
And rather comfort his distressed plight	*give him comfort in his agony and distress rather*

Than prosecute the meanest or the best
For these contempts. [Aside] Why, thus it shall become
High-witted Tamora to gloze with all.

But, Titus, I have touch'd thee to the quick,
Thy life-blood out; if Aaron now be wise,

Then is all safe, the anchor in the port.
Enter CLOWN
How now, good fellow! Wouldst thou speak with us?

CLOWN.
Yes, forsooth, an your mistressship be Emperial.

TAMORA.
Empress I am, but yonder sits the Emperor.

CLOWN.
'Tis he.- God and Saint Stephen give you godden. I have
brought you a letter and a couple of pigeons here.

[SATURNINUS reads the letter]

SATURNINUS.
Go take him away, and hang him presently.

CLOWN.
How much money must I have?

TAMORA.
Come, sirrah, you must be hang'd.

CLOWN.
Hang'd! by'r lady, then I have brought up a neck to a fair end.
[Exit guarded]

SATURNINUS.
Despiteful and intolerable wrongs!
Shall I endure this monstrous villainy?
I know from whence this same device proceeds.
May this be borne- as if his traitorous sons

That died by law for murder of our brother

---

than prosecute the highest or lowest
for these libels. [Aside] So, it shall look as though

noble spirited Tamora has a good word for everyone.
But, Titus, I have stabbed you to the heart, your blood is running out; if Aaron plays his part well now,
then everything is well, we're settled.

Hello there, good fellow! Do you want to speak to us?

Yes indeed, if your ladyship is imperial.

I am the Empress, but the Emperor is over there.

That's the one. By God and Saint Stephen I wish you good
evening. I have brought you a letter and a couple of pigeons here.

Take him away, and hang him quickly.

How much am I to be paid?

Come, sir, you are going to be hanged.

Hanged! By heaven, this is a nice way to finish matters.

Spiteful and intolerable wrongs!
Do I have to put up with this shocking villainy?
I know where this message comes from.
Do I have to put up with this - as if his traitorous sons
who were lawfully executed for the murder of my

Have by my means been butchered wrongfully?
Go drag the villain hithcr by the hair;
Nor age nor honour shall shape privilege.
For this proud mock I'll be thy slaughterman,
Sly frantic wretch, that holp'st to make me great,
In hope thyself should govern Rome and me.

Enter NUNTIUS AEMILIUS
What news with thee, Aemilius?

AEMILIUS.
Arm, my lords! Rome never had more cause.

The Goths have gathered head; and with a power

Of high resolved men, bent to the spoil,
They hither march amain, under conduct
Of Lucius, son to old Andronicus;
Who threats in course of this revenge to do
As much as ever Coriolanus did.

SATURNINUS.
Is warlike Lucius general of the Goths?
These tidings nip me, and I hang the head
As flowers with frost, or grass beat down with
storms.
Ay, now begins our sorrows to approach.
'Tis he the common people love so much;
Myself hath often heard them say-
When I have walked like a private man-
That Lucius' banishment was wrongfully,
And they have wish'd that Lucius were their
emperor.
TAMORA.
Why should you fear? Is not your city strong?

SATURNINUS.
Ay, but the citizens favour Lucius,
And will revolt from me to succour him.

TAMORA.
King, be thy thoughts imperious like thy name!
Is the sun dimm'd, that gnats do fly in it?
The eagle suffers little birds to sing,
And is not careful what they mean thereby,
Knowing that with the shadow of his wings

brother,
have been unjustly slaughtered by me?
Go and drag the villain in here by the hair;
neither his age nor position will protect him.
For this arrogant mockery I'll be your executioner,
cunning mad wretch, who wanted to promote me
in the hope that you could rule over both Rome and
me.

What news do you have, Aemilius?

Arm yourselves, my lords! Rome never needed to
more.
The Goths have raised their army, and they are
marching
here under full steam, with a force of resolute men,
determined to taste victory, under the leadership
of Lucius, the son of old Andronicus;
he threatens in taking his revenge to do
as much as Coriolanus ever did.

Is the warlike Lucius leading the Goths?
This news depresses me, and I hang down my head
like flowers in the frost, or grass flattened by the
storms.
Yes, now the bad times are coming.
He's the one the common people adore;
I've often heard them say myself -
when I've gone around in disguise -
that Lucius was wrongfully banished,
and they wished he was their Emperor.

Why be afraid? Isn't your city strong?

Yes, but the citizens favour Lucius,
and will rebel against me to support him.

King, in your thoughts live up to your name!
Is the sun dimmed if gnats fly across it?
The eagle allows the little birds to sing
and doesn't care what they're saying,
knowing that he can stop their song whenever he
likes

He can at pleasure stint their melody;
Even so mayest thou the giddy men of Rome.

Then cheer thy spirit; for know thou, Emperor,
I will enchant the old Andronicus
With words more sweet, and yet more dangerous,
Than baits to fish or honey-stalks to sheep,
When as the one is wounded with the bait,
The other rotted with delicious feed.

just by showing the shadow of his wings;
that's how you can deal with the changeable men of
Rome.
So cheer up; for you should know, Emperor,
I will enchant old Andronicus
with words that are sweeter, but more dangerous,
than bait to fish or clover to sheep,
when one is wounded with the bait,
and the other is sickened with the delicious food.

SATURNINUS.
But he will not entreat his son for us.

But he will not try to stop his son for us.

TAMORA.
If Tamora entreat him, then he will;
For I can smooth and fill his aged ears
With golden promises, that, were his heart
Almost impregnable, his old ears deaf,
Yet should both ear and heart obey my tongue.

He will if I ask him to;
for I can calm him and fill his old ears
with such golden promises that if his heart
was almost impermeable, his old ears deaf,
his ears would still hear me and his heart still obey
me.

[To AEMILIUS] Go thou before to be our
ambassador;
Say that the Emperor requests a parley
Of warlike Lucius, and appoint the meeting
Even at his father's house, the old Andronicus.

You go ahead as my ambassador;

say that the Emperor wants a meeting
with warlike Lucius, and arrange the meeting
at the house of his father, old Andronicus.

SATURNINUS.
Aemilius, do this message honourably;
And if he stand on hostage for his safety,
Bid him demand what pledge will please him best.

Aemilius, carry this message faithfully;
if he asks for guarantees of his safety,
tell him to ask for whatever promise best suits him.

AEMILIUS.
Your bidding shall I do effectually.
Exit

I shall carry out your orders to the letter.

TAMORA.
Now will I to that old Andronicus,
And temper him with all the art I have,
To pluck proud Lucius from the warlike Goths.
And now, sweet Emperor, be blithe again,
And bury all thy fear in my devices

Now I will go to that old Andronicus,
and persuade him with all the tricks I know,
to separate proud Lucius from the warlike Goths.
And now, sweet Emperor, be happy again,
and forget your fear, have faith in my plans.

SATURNINUS.
Then go successantly, and plead to him.

Then follow our ambassador, and go and persuade
him.

Exeunt

ACT V

SCENE I. Plains near Rome

Enter LUCIUS with an army of GOTHS with drums and colours

LUCIUS.

Approved warriors and my faithful friends,	*Proven warriors and my faithful friends,*
I have received letters from great Rome	*I have received letters from great Rome*
Which signifies what hate they bear their Emperor	*which show what hate they have for their Emperor*
And how desirous of our sight they are.	*and how much they what to see us arrive.*
Therefore, great lords, be, as your titles witness,	*So, great lords, live up to your great titles,*
Imperious and impatient of your wrongs;	*be imperial and don't suffer any wrongs;*
And wherein Rome hath done you any scath,	*wherever Rome has done you any harm,*
Let him make treble satisfaction.	*pay him back in triplicate.*

FIRST GOTH.

Brave slip, sprung from the great Andronicus,	*Brave offshoot, sprung from the great Andronicus,*
Whose name was once our terror, now our comfort,	*whose name was once a terror to us, is now our help,*
Whose high exploits and honourable deeds	*whose great adventures and honourable deeds*
Ingrateful Rome requites with foul contempt,	*ungrateful Rome repays with foul contempt,*
Be bold in us: we'll follow where thou lead'st,	*have confidence in us: we'll follow where you lead,*
Like stinging bees in hottest summer's day,	*like stinging bees on the hottest summer's day,*
Led by their master to the flow'red fields,	*led by their ruler to the rich fields,*
And be aveng'd on cursed Tamora.	*and we will have revenge on cursed Tamora.*

ALL THE GOTHS.

And as he saith, so say we all with him.	*We all second what he says.*

LUCIUS.

I humbly thank him, and I thank you all.	*I give him my humble thanks, and the same to you all.*
But who comes here, led by a lusty Goth?	*But who's this coming, led by a strong Goth?*

Enter a GOTH, leading AARON with his CHILD in his arms

SECOND GOTH.

Renowned Lucius, from our troops I stray'd	*Honoured Lucius, I strayed away from our troops*
To gaze upon a ruinous monastery;	*to look at a tumbledown monastery;*
And as I earnestly did fix mine eye	*and as I looked closely at*
Upon the wasted building, suddenly	*the ruined building, suddenly*
I heard a child cry underneath a wall.	*I heard a child crying behind a wall.*
I made unto the noise, when soon I heard	*I headed for the noise, and I soon heard*
The crying babe controll'd with this discourse:	*the crying baby calmed with these words;*
'Peace, tawny slave, half me and half thy dam!	*"Quiet, brown slave, half me and half your mother!*
Did not thy hue bewray whose brat thou art,	*If your colour didn't show whose brat you are,*
Had nature lent thee but thy mother's look,	*if nature had just given you your mother's looks,*
Villain, thou mightst have been an emperor;	*villain, you could have been an Emperor;*

But where the bull and cow are both milk-white,
They never do beget a coal-black calf.
Peace, villain, peace!- even thus he rates the babe-

'For I must bear thee to a trusty Goth,
Who, when he knows thou art the Empress' babe,

Will hold thee dearly for thy mother's sake.'
With this, my weapon drawn, I rush'd upon him,
Surpris'd him suddenly, and brought him hither
To use as you think needful of the man.

but when the bull and the cow are both snow white,
they never have a coal-black calf.
Quiet, villain, quiet!" - that's how he spoke to the
baby -
"For I must take you to a trusty Goth,
who, when he knows you are the child of the
Empress,
will look after you well for your mother's sake."
At that I rushed at him with my sword out,
took him by surprise and brought him here
to do with as you see fit.

LUCIUS.
O worthy Goth, this is the incarnate devil
That robb'd Andronicus of his good hand;
This is the pearl that pleas'd your Empress' eye;
And here's the base fruit of her burning lust.
Say, wall-ey'd slave, whither wouldst thou convey
This growing image of thy fiend-like face?
Why dost not speak? What, deaf? Not a word?

A halter, soldiers! Hang him on this tree,
And by his side his fruit of bastardy.

Good Goth, this is the bloody devil
who robbed Andronicus of his worthy hand;
this is the pearl that took your Empress' fancy;
and here's the low offspring of her burning lust.
Tell us, glaring slave, where were you taking
this living copy of your devilish face?
Why don't you speak? What, are you deaf? Not a
word?
Bring a rope, soldiers! Hang him on this tree,
and hang his bastard child next to him.

AARON.
Touch not the boy, he is of royal blood.

Don't touch the boy, he has royal blood in him.

LUCIUS.
Too like the sire for ever being good.
First hang the child, that he may see it sprawl-
A sight to vex the father's soul withal.
Get me a ladder.
[A ladder brought, which AARON is made to climb]

He's too like his father to ever be any good.
Hang the child first, so he can see it die-
a sight to torment a father's soul.
Get me a ladder.

AARON.
Lucius, save the child,
And bear it from me to the Emperess.
If thou do this, I'll show thee wondrous things
That highly may advantage thee to hear;
If thou wilt not, befall what may befall,
I'll speak no more but 'Vengeance rot you all!'

Lucius, spare the child,
and carry it from me to the Empress.
If you do this, I'll tell you amazing things,
that will be greatly to your advantage;
if you won't, whatever happens
all I'll say will be, "May you all rot in hell!"

LUCIUS.
Say on; an if it please me which thou speak'st,
Thy child shall live, and I will see it nourish'd.

Carry on; if I'm pleased with what you say,
your child shall live, and I will treat it well.

AARON.

An if it please thee! Why, assure thee, Lucius,
'Twill vex thy soul to hear what I shall speak;

For I must talk of murders, rapes, and massacres,

Acts of black night, abominable deeds,
Complots of mischief, treason, villainies,
Ruthful to hear, yet piteously perform'd;
And this shall all be buried in my death,
Unless thou swear to me my child shall live.

LUCIUS.
Tell on thy mind; I say thy child shall live.

AARON.
Swear that he shall, and then I will begin.

LUCIUS.
Who should I swear by? Thou believest no god;

That granted, how canst thou believe an oath?

AARON.
What if I do not? as indeed I do not;
Yet, for I know thou art religious
And hast a thing within thee called conscience,
With twenty popish tricks and ceremonies
Which I have seen thee careful to observe,
Therefore I urge thy oath. For that I know
An idiot holds his bauble for a god,
And keeps the oath which by that god he swears,
To that I'll urge him. Therefore thou shalt vow
By that same god- what god soe'er it be
That thou adorest and hast in reverence-
To save my boy, to nourish and bring him up;
Or else I will discover nought to thee.

LUCIUS.
Even by my god I swear to thee I will.

AARON.
First know thou, I begot him on the Empress.

LUCIUS.
O most insatiate and luxurious woman!

AARON.

*If you're pleased! I can assure you, Lucius,
that it will torture your soul to hear what I have to say;*

*I have to tell you about murders, rapes and massacres,
devilish acts, horrible deeds,
mischievous plots, treason, villainy,
sad to hear of, but inspiring pity;
and all this will go with me to the grave,
unless you swear to me my child shall live.*

Say what you know; I say your child shall live.

Swear that he will, and I'll begin.

*Who should I swear by? You don't believe in any god;
given that, how can you believe in any oath?*

*So what if I don't? I certainly don't;
but I know that you are religious,
and have that thing called conscience inside you.
I've seen you carefully carry out
lots of different forms of worship,
and so I ask you to swear. If I know that
an idiot worships a stick,
and keeps his promise when he swears by that god,
I'll ask him to do it. So you will promise
by that god - whatever god it may be -
that you worship and adore -
to save my boy, to feed him and raise him;
otherwise I'll tell you nothing.*

I swear by my god that I will.

Firstly you should know, I fathered him with the Empress.

Oh, what an insatiable and lecherous woman!

Original	Modern
Tut, Lucius, this was but a deed of charity To that which thou shalt hear of me anon. 'Twas her two sons that murdered Bassianus; They cut thy sister's tongue, and ravish'd her, And cut her hands, and trimm'd her as thou sawest.	Tut, Lucius, that would seem like a charitable deed compared to what you'll hear from me soon. It was her two sons who murdered Bassanius; they cut your sister's tongue out, and raped her, and cut her hands off, pruning her as you saw.

LUCIUS.

| O detestable villain! Call'st thou that trimming? | You horrible villain! You call that pruning? |

AARON.

| Why, she was wash'd, and cut, and trimm'd, and 'twas
Trim sport for them which had the doing of it. | Well, she was, washed, cut and pruned, and it was
good fun for the ones who did it. |

LUCIUS.

| O barbarous beastly villains like thyself! | Barbarous beastly villains like you! |

AARON.

| Indeed, I was their tutor to instruct them.
That codding spirit had they from their mother,
As sure a card as ever won the set;
That bloody mind, I think, they learn'd of me,
As true a dog as ever fought at head.
Well, let my deeds be witness of my worth.
I train'd thy brethren to that guileful hole
Where the dead corpse of Bassianus lay;
I wrote the letter that thy father found,
And hid the gold within that letter mention'd,
Confederate with the Queen and her two sons;
And what not done, that thou hast cause to rue,
Wherein I had no stroke of mischief in it?
I play'd the cheater for thy father's hand,
And, when I had it, drew myself apart
And almost broke my heart with extreme laughter.
I pried me through the crevice of a wall,
When, for his hand, he had his two sons' heads;
Beheld his tears, and laugh'd so heartily
That both mine eyes were rainy like to his;
And when I told the Empress of this sport,
She swooned almost at my pleasing tale,
And for my tidings gave me twenty kisses. | That's right, I was the one who taught them.
They got their lecherous spirit from their mother,
she guaranteed they would be like that;
their murderousness they learned from me, I think,
as good a dog as ever attacked head on.
Well, let my deeds show what I'm worth.
I enticed your brothers to that evil pit
where the dead corpse of Bassanius lay;
I wrote the letter which your father found,
and hid the gold that was mentioned in that letter,
as part of a plot with the Queen and her two sons;
is there anything which has caused you pain
which I didn't have a wicked hand in?
I played the trick which won your father's hand,
and, when I won it, I drew aside
and almost burst my heart laughing.
I spied through a crack in a wall
when he got his two sons' heads in exchange;
I saw his tears and laughed so much
that both my eyes were full of tears like his;
and when I told the empress of this fun,
she almost fainted with pleasure at the story,
and gave me twenty kisses for the news. |

GOTH.

| What, canst thou say all this and never blush? | What, can you say all this and not blush? |

AARON.

| Ay, like a black dog, as the saying is. | Yes, like a black dog, as the saying has it. |

LUCIUS.
Art thou not sorry for these heinous deeds?

Aren't you sorry for the bad things you've done?

AARON.
Ay, that I had not done a thousand more

Yes, I'm sorry I hadn't done a thousand things more..

Even now I curse the day- and yet, I think,
Few come within the compass of my curse-
Wherein I did not some notorious ill;
As kill a man, or else devise his death;
Ravish a maid, or plot the way to do it;
Accuse some innocent, and forswear myself;

*Even now I curse any day - although I think
that there were very few I had to curse -
when I didn't do some terrible wrong;
like killing a man, or plotting his death;
raping a girl, or planning how to do it;
accusing some innocent person, and perjuring
myself;*

Set deadly enmity between two friends;
Make poor men's cattle break their necks;
Set fire on barns and hay-stacks in the night,
And bid the owners quench them with their tears.

*starting a deadly quarrel between two friends;
making poor men's cattle break their necks;
setting barns and haystacks on fire at night,
and telling the owners to put the fire out with their
tears.*

Oft have I digg'd up dead men from their graves,
And set them upright at their dear friends' door
Even when their sorrows almost was forgot,
And on their skins, as on the bark of trees,
Have with my knife carved in Roman letters
'Let not your sorrow die, though I am dead.'
Tut, I have done a thousand dreadful things
As willingly as one would kill a fly;
And nothing grieves me heartily indeed
But that I cannot do ten thousand more.

*I've often dug dead men up from their graves,
and stood them up at their dear family's door
when they had almost got over their loss,
and on their skins, like on the bark of trees,
I've carved, in Roman script, with my knife,
"Don't let your sorrow die, even though I'm dead."
Tcha, I have done a thousand dreadful things,
as easily as one would kill a fly;
nothing makes me so sad
that I can't do another thousand.*

LUCIUS.
Bring down the devil, for he must not die
So sweet a death as hanging presently.

*Bring the devil down, for he must not die
such an easy death as instant hanging.*

AARON.
If there be devils, would I were a devil,
To live and burn in everlasting fire,
So I might have your company in hell
But to torment you with my bitter tongue!

*If there are devils, I wish I was a devil,
to live and burn in eternal flames,
so I could have you with me in hell,
just to torture you with my bitter tongue!*

LUCIUS.
Sirs, stop his mouth, and let him speak no more.
Enter AEMILIUS

Sirs, gag him, don't let him say anything else.

GOTH.
My lord, there is a messenger from Rome
Desires to be admitted to your presence.

*My lord, there is a messenger from Rome
who wants to be let in to see you.*

LUCIUS.

Let him come near.
Welcome, Aemilius. What's the news from Rome?

AEMILIUS.
Lord Lucius, and you Princes of the Goths,
The Roman Emperor greets you all by me;

And, for he understands you are in arms,
He craves a parley at your father's house,
Willing you to demand your hostages,
And they shall be immediately deliver'd.

FIRST GOTH.
What says our general?

LUCIUS.
Aemilius, let the Emperor give his pledges
Unto my father and my uncle Marcus
And we will come. March away.
Exeunt

Let him in.
Welcome Aemilius. What's the news from Rome?

Lord Lucius, and you Princes of the Goths,
the Roman Emperor sends you all greetings through me;
and, as he knows you have gathered an army,
he wants a meeting at your father's house,
telling you to say what hostages you want,
and they shall be given to you at once.

What does our general say?

Aemilius, let the Emperor give his guarantees
to my father and my uncle Marcus
and we will come. March away.

SCENE II. Rome. Before TITUS' house

Enter TAMORA, and her two sons, DEMETRIUS and CHIRON, disguised

TAMORA.
Thus, in this strange and sad habiliment,
I will encounter with Andronicus,
And say I am Revenge, sent from below
To join with him and right his heinous wrongs.
Knock at his study, where they say he keeps
To ruminate strange plots of dire revenge;
Tell him Revenge is come to join with him,
And work confusion on his enemies.
They knock and TITUS opens his study door, above

So, in this unusual and dark clothing,
I will meet Andronicus,
and say I am Revenge, sent from below
to join him and right his terrible wrongs.
Knock on his study door, where they say he sits
brooding over strange plots of terrible revenge;
tell him Revenge has come to join him,
and wreak havoc on his enemies.

TITUS.
Who doth molest my contemplation?
Is it your trick to make me ope the door,
That so my sad decrees may fly away
And all my study be to no effect?
You are deceiv'd; for what I mean to do
See here in bloody lines I have set down;
And what is written shall be executed.

Who's disturbing my meditations?
Is this a trick to make me open the door,
so that my sad plans can be blown away,
and all my work be useless?
You are mistaken; I have written down
the bloody deeds I shall do,
and what is written down shall be done.

TAMORA.
Titus, I am come to talk with thee.

Titus, I have come to talk to you.

TITUS.
No, not a word. How can I grace my talk,
Wanting a hand to give it that accord?

Thou hast the odds of me; therefore no more.

No, not a word. What's the point in talking,
when I haven't got a hand to put whatever I say into
practice?
You have more hands to do things than I have; so
that's an end of it.

TAMORA.
If thou didst know me, thou wouldst talk with me.

If you knew who I was, you would talk to me.

TITUS.
I am not mad, I know thee well enough:
Witness this wretched stump, witness these crimson lines;
Witness these trenches made by grief and care;
Witness the tiring day and heavy night;

Witness all sorrow that I know thee well
For our proud Empress, mighty Tamora.

I am not mad, I know you perfectly well:
look at this wretched stump, look at these scars;

look at these lines scored by grief and care;
look at how tiring my days are, how heavy my
nights;
see all the sorrows which say I know that you are
our proud Empress, mighty Tamora.

Is not thy coming for my other hand?

You haven't come for my other hand?

TAMORA.
Know thou, sad man, I am not Tamora:
She is thy enemy and I thy friend.
I am Revenge, sent from th' infernal kingdom
To ease the gnawing vulture of thy mind
By working wreakful vengeance on thy foes.
Come down and welcome me to this world's light;
Confer with me of murder and of death;
There's not a hollow cave or lurking-place,
No vast obscurity or misty vale,
Where bloody murder or detested rape
Can couch for fear but I will find them out;
And in their ears tell them my dreadful name-
Revenge, which makes the foul offender quake.

You should know, sad man, I am not Tamora:
she is your enemy and I am your friend.
I am Revenge, sent from hell
to stop the anguish that's eating away at you
by wreaking vengeance on your enemies.
Come down and welcome me to your world;
speak to me about murder and death;
there's no cave or hiding place,
no great unknown plain or misty valley,
where bloody murder or horrible rape
can hide without being afraid that I'll find it out.
and whisper in their ears my dreadful name-
Revenge, which makes the foul criminal tremble.

TITUS.
Art thou Revenge? and art thou sent to me
To be a torment to mine enemies?

Are you revenge? And have you been sent to me
to torture my enemies?

TAMORA.
I am; therefore come down and welcome me.

I am, so come down and welcome me.

TITUS.
Do me some service ere I come to thee.
Lo, by thy side where Rape and Murder stands;

Now give some surance that thou art Revenge-
Stab them, or tear them on thy chariot wheels;

And then I'll come and be thy waggoner
And whirl along with thee about the globes.
Provide thee two proper palfreys, black as jet,
To hale thy vengeful waggon swift away,
And find out murderers in their guilty caves;
And when thy car is loaden with their heads,
I will dismount, and by thy waggon wheel
Trot, like a servile footman, all day long,
Even from Hyperion's rising in the east
Until his very downfall in the sea.
And day by day I'll do this heavy task,
So thou destroy Rapine and Murder there.

Do something for me before I join you.
See where Rape and Murder are standing at your side;
now give me some proof that you are Revenge -
stab them, or pull them to pieces with your chariot wheels;
and then I'll come and be your driver
and fly among the stars with you.
Provide two good horses, black as night,
to pull your vengeful wagon at great speed
and find the murderers in their guilty hideouts;
and when your carriage is loaded with their heads
I will get down and trot along by the side
of your carriage like a servile footman all day long,
from the moment the sun rises in the east
until he sets in the sea.
I'll do this onerous task every day,
as long as you destroy Rape and Murder, who are standing there.

TAMORA.
These are my ministers, and come with me.

These are my ministers, and they have come with me.

91

TITUS.
Are they thy ministers? What are they call'd?

They are your ministers? What are they called?

TAMORA.
Rape and Murder; therefore called so
'Cause they take vengeance of such kind of men.

Rape and murder; they are called that because that's the type of revenge they take on mankind.

TITUS.
Good Lord, how like the Empress' sons they are!

And you the Empress! But we worldly men
Have miserable, mad, mistaking eyes.
O sweet Revenge, now do I come to thee;
And, if one arm's embracement will content thee,
I will embrace thee in it by and by.

Good lord, how similar they are to the Empress' sons!
And you to the Empress! But we earthly men, have weak, mad, error-prone eyes.
Oh sweet Revenge, I'm coming to you; and if being embraced by one arm is enough for you I will embrace you with it shortly.

TAMORA.
This closing with him fits his lunacy.
Whate'er I forge to feed his brain-sick humours,
Do you uphold and maintain in your speeches,
For now he firmly takes me for Revenge;
And, being credulous in this mad thought,
I'll make him send for Lucius his son,
And whilst I at a banquet hold him sure,
I'll find some cunning practice out of hand
To scatter and disperse the giddy Goths,
Or, at the least, make them his enemies.
See, here he comes, and I must ply my theme.
Enter TITUS, below

This agreement with him shows he is mad.
Whatever I make up to feed his madness, you play along with it in what you say, because he now really thinks I am Revenge; now he's convinced by this mad idea, I'll make him send for his son Lucius, and whilst I keep him, convinced, at a banquet, I'll improvise some cunning plan to scatter and disperse the volatile Goths. Or, at least, make them his enemies. See, here he comes, and I must carry on my deceit.

TITUS.
Long have I been forlorn, and all for thee.
Welcome, dread Fury, to my woeful house.
Rapine and Murder, you are welcome too.
How like the Empress and her sons you are!
Well are you fitted, had you but a Moor.
Could not all hell afford you such a devil?
For well I wot the Empress never wags
But in her company there is a Moor;
And, would you represent our queen aright,
It were convenient you had such a devil.
But welcome as you are. What shall we do?

I have been alone for a long time, waiting for you.
Welcome, terrible Goddess, to my sad house.
Rape and Murder, you are welcome too.
How like the Empress and her sons you are!
You'd be identical, if you just had a Moor with you.
Couldn't the whole of hell give you such a devil?
For I know very well the Empress never goes anywhere without her Moor with her; if you wanted to give a true imitation of our queen, you ought to have such a devil with you. But you are welcome as you are. What shall we do?

TAMORA.
What wouldst thou have us do, Andronicus?

What do you want us to do, Andronicus?

DEMETRIUS.
Show me a murderer, I'll deal with him.

Show me a murderer, I'll deal with him.

CHIRON.
Show me a villain that hath done a rape,
And I am sent to be reveng'd on him.

Show me a villain who has committed rape,
I am here to take revenge on him.

TAMORA.
Show me a thousand that hath done thee wrong,
And I will be revenged on them all.

Show me a thousand who have done you wrong,
and I will take revenge on all of them.

TITUS.
Look round about the wicked streets of Rome,
And when thou find'st a man that's like thyself,

Good Murder, stab him; he's a murderer.
Go thou with him, and when it is thy hap
To find another that is like to thee,
Good Rapine, stab him; he is a ravisher.
Go thou with them; and in the Emperor's court
There is a queen, attended by a Moor;
Well shalt thou know her by thine own proportion,
For up and down she doth resemble thee.
I pray thee, do on them some violent death;
They have been violent to me and mine.

Look around the streets wicked streets of Rome,
and, good Murder, when you find a man that looks like you,
stab him; he's a murderer.
Go with him good Rape, and when you have the luck
to find another who looks like you,
stab him; he's a rapist.
You go with them; in the Emperor's court
there's a queen, with a Moor waiting on her;
you'll know her through her resemblance to you which is exact.
Please, make them suffer some violent death;
they have done violence to me and my family.

TAMORA.
Well hast thou lesson'd us; this shall we do.

But would it please thee, good Andronicus,
To send for Lucius, thy thrice-valiant son,
Who leads towards Rome a band of warlike Goths,

And bid him come and banquet at thy house;
When he is here, even at thy solemn feast,

I will bring in the Empress and her sons,
The Emperor himself, and all thy foes;
And at thy mercy shall they stoop and kneel,
And on them shalt thou ease thy angry heart.
What says Andronicus to this device?

You have given us clear instructions; we shall do this.
But how would you feel, good Andronicus,
about sending for Lucius, your triply valiant son,
who is leading a band of warlike Goths towards Rome,
and asking him to come to a banquet at your house;
when he is here, in the middle of your dignified feast,
I will bring in the Empress and her sons,
the Emperor himself and all your enemies;
they shall bow and scrape to ask you for mercy,
and you shall take out your anger on them.
What does Andronicus say to this plan?

TITUS.
Marcus, my brother! 'Tis sad Titus calls.
Enter MARCUS
Go, gentle Marcus, to thy nephew Lucius;
Thou shalt inquire him out among the Goths.
Bid him repair to me, and bring with him

Marcus, my brother! Sad Titus is calling you.

Go, gentle Marcus, to your nephew Lucius;
you shall seek him out amongst the Goths.
Tell him to come to me, and bring with him

Some of the chiefest princes of the Goths;
Bid him encamp his soldiers where they are.
Tell him the Emperor and the Empress too
Feast at my house, and he shall feast with them.
This do thou for my love; and so let him,

As he regards his aged father's life.

MARCUS.
This will I do, and soon return again.
Exit

TAMORA.
Now will I hence about thy business,
And take my ministers along with me.

TITUS.
Nay, nay, let Rape and Murder stay with me,
Or else I'll call my brother back again,
And cleave to no revenge but Lucius.

TAMORA. [Aside to her sons]
What say you, boys? Will you
abide
with him,
Whiles I go tell my lord the Emperor
How I have govern'd our determin'd jest?
Yield to his humour, smooth and speak him fair,

And tarry with him till I turn again.

TITUS. [Aside]
I knew them all, though they suppos'd me mad,

And will o'er reach them in their own devices,
A pair of cursed hell-hounds and their dam.

DEMETRIUS.
Madam, depart at pleasure; leave us here.

TAMORA.
Farewell, Andronicus, Revenge now goes
To lay a complot to betray thy foes.

TITUS.
I know thou dost; and, sweet Revenge, farewell.
  Exit TAMORA

some of the greatest princes of the Goths;
tell him to leave his soldiers camped where they are.
Tell him that the Emperor and the Empress too
are eating at my house, and he shall eat with them.
Do this out of love for me, and tell him to do it for
the same reason,
out of respect for his elderly father.

I'll do this, and be back soon.

Now I'll go about my business,
and take my ministers along with me.

No, no, let Rape and Murder stay with me,
otherwise I'll call my brother back,
and let Lucius be the one who takes revenge for me.

What do you say, boys? Will you stay with him

whilst I go to tell my lord the Emperor
how I have carried out our plans?
Play along with his madness, calm him and speak
sweetly,
and keep him occupied until I come back.

I knew who they were, though they thought I was
mad,
and I'll beat them at their own game,
a pair of cursed hellhounds and their mother.

Madam, leave when you wish; we'll stay here.

Farewell, Andronicus, Revenge is now going
to start a plot to bring down your enemies.

I know you are, and farewell to you, sweet Revenge.

CHIRON.
Tell us, old man, how shall we be employ'd?

Tell us, old man, what do you what us to do?

TITUS.
Tut, I have work enough for you to do.
Publius, come hither, Caius, and Valentine.
Enter PUBLIUS, CAIUS, and VALENTINE

Come, I have enough work for you to do.
Publius, come here, Caius and Valentine.

PUBLIUS.
What is your will?

What do you wish?

TITUS.
Know you these two?

Do you know these two?

PUBLIUS.
The Empress' sons, I take them: Chiron, Demetrius.

They're the Empress' sons, I see; Chiron and Demetrius.

TITUS.
Fie, Publius, fie! thou art too much deceiv'd.
The one is Murder, and Rape is the other's name;
And therefore bind them, gentle Publius-
Caius and Valentine, lay hands on them.
Oft have you heard me wish for such an hour,
And now I find it; therefore bind them sure,
And stop their mouths if they begin to cry.

Don't be stupid, Publius! You have been tricked.
One is Murder and the other is called Rape;
so tie them up, gentle Publius-
Caius and Valentine, grab hold of them.
You've often heard me say I'd like this chance,
and now I have it; so tie them tight,
and gag them if they try to shout.

Exit
[They lay hold on CHIRON and DEMETRIUS]

CHIRON.
Villains, forbear! we are the Empress' sons.

Villains, give over! We are the Empress' sons.

PUBLIUS.
And therefore do we what we are commanded.
Stop close their mouths, let them not speak a word.
Is he sure bound? Look that you bind them fast.
 Re-enter TITUS ANDRONICUS
with a knife, and LAVINIA, with a basin

And so we'll do what we were told.
Gag them tightly, don't let them say a word.
Is he well tied? Make sure the knots are fast.

TITUS.
Come, come, Lavinia; look, thy foes are bound.
Sirs, stop their mouths, let them not speak to me;
But let them hear what fearful words I utter.
O villains, Chiron and Demetrius!
Here stands the spring whom you have stain'd
with mud;

Come, come, Lavinia; look, your enemies are tied up.
Sirs, gag them, don't let them speak to me;
but let them hear the fearsome things I have to say.
You villains, Chiron and Demetrius!
here is the spring which you have polluted with mud;

This goodly summer with your winter mix'd.
You kill'd her husband; and for that vile fault
Two of her brothers were condemn'd to death,
My hand cut off and made a merry jest;
Both her sweet hands, her tongue, and that more dear
Than hands or tongue, her spotless chastity,
Inhuman traitors, you constrain'd and forc'd.

What would you say, if I should let you speak?
Villains, for shame you could not beg for grace.

Hark, wretches! how I mean to martyr you.
This one hand yet is left to cut your throats,
Whiles that Lavinia 'tween her stumps doth hold
The basin that receives your guilty blood.
You know your mother means to feast with me,
And calls herself Revenge, and thinks me mad.
Hark, villains! I will grind your bones to dust,
And with your blood and it I'll make a paste;
And of the paste a coffin I will rear,
And make two pasties of your shameful heads;
And bid that strumpet, your unhallowed dam,
Like to the earth, swallow her own increase.
This is the feast that I have bid her to,
And this the banquet she shall surfeit on;
For worse than Philomel you us'd my daughter,

And worse than Progne I will be reveng'd.
And now prepare your throats. Lavinia, come,
Receive the blood; and when that they are dead,
Let me go grind their bones to powder small,
And with this hateful liquor temper it;
And in that paste let their vile heads be bak'd.
Come, come, be every one officious
To make this banquet, which I wish may prove
More stern and bloody than the Centaurs' feast.

[He cuts their throats]
So.
Now bring them in, for I will play the cook,
And see them ready against their mother comes.
Exeunt, bearing the dead bodies

the sweet summer which you mixed with winter.
You killed her husband, and for that evil crime
two of her brothers were condemned to death,
and my hand was cut of to mock me;
you inhuman traitors held her down and stole

both of her sweet hands, her tongue,
and the thing more important to her
than both, her unblemished chastity.
What would you say, if I let you speak?
Villains, you wouldn't have the nerve to beg for mercy.
Listen, wretches! I'll tell you how I mean to kill you.
I have this one hand left to cut your throats,
while Lavinia holds the basin between her stumps
which will collect your guilty blood.
You know your mother intends to come to my feast,
and calls herself Revenge, and thinks I am mad.
Listen, villains! I will grind your bones into dust,
and I'll mix it into a paste with your blood,
and I'll make a piecrust of that paste,
and make two pies out of your sinful heads;
I'll ask that strumpet, your unholy mother,
to swallow her own produce, she'll be your grave.
This is the feast I have invited her to,
and the banquet she shall be stuffed with;
for you have treated my daughter worse than Philomel,
and I will take a worse revenge than Progne.
Now prepare your throats. Lavinia, come,
collect the blood; and when they are dead,
Let me go and grind their bones to fine powder
and mix it with this foul liquid,
and let their foul heads be baked in that paste.
Come, come, let everyone get busy
in arranging this banquet, which I hope will
prove to be more stern and bloody than the Centaur's feast.

It's done.
Now bring them in, for I will be the cook,
and have them prepared for their mother's arrival.

SCENE III. The court of TITUS' house

Enter Lucius, MARCUS, and the GOTHS, with AARON prisoner, and his CHILD in the arms of an attendant

LUCIUS.
Uncle Marcus, since 'tis my father's mind
That I repair to Rome, I am content.

*Uncle Marcus, as it's my father's wish
that I return to Rome, I am happy to do so.*

FIRST GOTH.
And ours with thine, befall what fortune will.

*And we're happy to go along with whatever you
decide,whatever happens.*

LUCIUS.
Good uncle, take you in this barbarous Moor,

This ravenous tiger, this accursed devil;
Let him receive no sust'nance, fetter him,
Till he be brought unto the Empress' face

For testimony of her foul proceedings.
And see the ambush of our friends be strong;
I fear the Emperor means no good to us.

*Good uncle, take this barbarous Moor into your
custody,
this ravenous tiger, this cursed devil;
don't feed him, chain him,
until he can be brought face to face with the
Empress
as a witness to her foul behaviour.
Make sure our forces are strong;
I fear the Emperor means to do us harm.*

AARON.
Some devil whisper curses in my ear,
And prompt me that my tongue may utter forth
The venomous malice of my swelling heart!

*I'd like some devil to whisper curses in my ear,
giving me inspiration to speak out
the poisonous evil in my swollen heart!*

LUCIUS.
Away, inhuman dog, unhallowed slave!
Sirs, help our uncle to convey him in.
Exeunt GOTHS with AARON. Flourish within
The trumpets show the Emperor is at hand.
Sound trumpets. Enter SATURNINUS and
TAMORA, with AEMILIUS, TRIBUNES, SENATORS, and others

*Away with you, inhuman dog, unholy slave!
Gentlemen, help my uncle take him away.*

The trumpets show the Emperor is nearby.

SATURNINUS.
What, hath the firmament more suns than one?

What's this, is there more than one sun in the sky?

LUCIUS.
What boots it thee to call thyself a sun?

What use is it to call yourself a sun?

MARCUS.
Rome's Emperor, and nephew, break the parle;

These quarrels must be quietly debated.
The feast is ready which the careful Titus
Hath ordain'd to an honourable end,
For peace, for love, for league, and good to Rome.
Please you, therefore, draw nigh and take your

*Rome's emperor, and you my nephew, start the
negotiations;
these arguments must be debated peacefully.
The feast is ready which the suffering Titus
has ordered for honourable purposes,
out of peace, love, alliance, and the good of Rome.
So please, come in and sit down.*

places.

SATURNINUS.
Marcus, we will.

Marcus, we will.

[A table brought in. The company sit down]
Trumpets sounding, enter TITUS
like a cook, placing the dishes, and LAVINIA
with a veil over her face; also YOUNG LUCIUS, and others

TITUS.
Welcome, my lord; welcome, dread Queen;
Welcome, ye warlike Goths; welcome, Lucius;
And welcome all. Although the cheer be poor,
'Twill fill your stomachs; please you eat of it.

Welcome, my lord; welcome, fearsome queen;
welcome, you warlike Goths; welcome, Lucius;
and welcome all. Although the food is humble,
it will fill your stomachs; please eat.

SATURNINUS.
Why art thou thus attir'd, Andronicus?

Why are you dressed like this, Andronicus?

TITUS.
Because I would be sure to have all well

Because I wanted to make sure that everything was suitable

To entertain your Highness and your Empress.

to welcome your Highness and your Empress.

TAMORA.
We are beholding to you, good Andronicus.

We are grateful to you, good Andronicus.

TITUS.
An if your Highness knew my heart, you were.
My lord the Emperor, resolve me this:
Was it well done of rash Virginius
To slay his daughter with his own right hand,
Because she was enforc'd, stain'd, and deflower'd?

If you knew what was in my heart you would be.
My lord the Emperor, explain this to me:
was hasty Virginius right
to kill his daughter with his own hand,
because she was trapped, dishonoured and deflowered?

SATURNINUS.
It was, Andronicus.

He was, Andronicus.

TITUS.
Your reason, mighty lord.

Why do you say that, mighty lord?

SATURNINUS.
Because the girl should not survive her shame,
And by her presence still renew his sorrows.

So that the girl would not live in shame,
and continually remind him of his sorrow.

TITUS.
A reason mighty, strong, and effectual;
A pattern, precedent, and lively warrant

A great reason, strong and logical;
an example, precedent and striking permission

98

For me, most wretched, to perform the like.
Die, die, Lavinia, and thy shame with thee;
 [He kills her]
And with thy shame thy father's sorrow die!

for me, the most wretched man, to do the same.
Die, die, Lavinia, and let your shame die with you;
 [he kills her]
and let your father's sorrow die with your shame!

SATURNINUS.
What hast thou done, unnatural and unkind?

What have you done, you unnatural and horrible man?

TITUS.
Kill'd her for whom my tears have made me blind.

I've killed the one who was causing the tears which made me blind.

I am as woeful as Virginius was,
And have a thousand times more cause than he
To do this outrage; and it now is done.

I am as sad as Virginius was,
and have a thousand times more reason
to do this awful thing; now it's done.

SATURNINUS.
What, was she ravish'd? Tell who did the deed.

What, was she raped? Tell me who did it.

TITUS.
Will't please you eat? Will't please your Highness feed?

Would you like to eat? Would your Highnesses please tuck in?

TAMORA.
Why hast thou slain thine only daughter thus?

Why have you killed your only daughter like this?

TITUS.
Not I; 'twas Chiron and Demetrius.
They ravish'd her, and cut away her tongue;
And they, 'twas they, that did her all this wrong.

It wasn't me; it was Chiron and Demetrius.
They raped her and cut out her tongue;
and they were the ones who killed her.

SATURNINUS.
Go, fetch them hither to us presently.

Go, bring them here to us at once.

TITUS.
Why, there they are, both baked in this pie,
Whereof their mother daintily hath fed,
Eating the flesh that she herself hath bred.
'Tis true, 'tis true: witness my knife's sharp point.

Why, there they are, both baked in this pie,
which their mother has just enjoyed,
eating the flesh she bred herself.
It's true, it's true: let my sharp knifepoint be my witness.

[He stabs the EMPRESS]

SATURNINUS.
Die, frantic wretch, for this accursed deed!
[He stabs TITUS]

Die, mad wretch, for this cursed deed!

LUCIUS.
Can the son's eye behold his father bleed?
There's meed for meed, death for a deadly deed.
[He stabs SATURNINUS. A great tumult. LUCIUS,
MARCUS, and their friends go up into the balcony]

MARCUS.
You sad-fac'd men, people and sons of Rome,
By uproars sever'd, as a flight of fowl
Scatter'd by winds and high tempestuous gusts,
O, let me teach you how to knit again
This scattered corn into one mutual sheaf,
These broken limbs again into one body;
Lest Rome herself be bane unto herself,
And she whom mighty kingdoms curtsy to,
Like a forlorn and desperate castaway,
Do shameful execution on herself.
But if my frosty signs and chaps of age,
Grave witnesses of true experience,
Cannot induce you to attend my words,
[To Lucius] Speak, Rome's dear friend, as erst our
 ancestor,
When with his solemn tongue he did discourse
To love-sick Dido's sad attending ear
The story of that baleful burning night,
When subtle Greeks surpris'd King Priam's Troy.

Tell us what Sinon hath bewitch'd our ears,
Or who hath brought the fatal engine in
That gives our Troy, our Rome, the civil wound.
My heart is not compact of flint nor steel;
Nor can I utter all our bitter grief,
But floods of tears will drown my oratory
And break my utt'rance, even in the time
When it should move ye to attend me most,
And force you to commiseration.
Here's Rome's young Captain, let him tell the tale;

While I stand by and weep to hear him speak.

LUCIUS.
Then, gracious auditory, be it known to you
That Chiron and the damn'd Demetrius
Were they that murd'red our Emperor's brother;
And they it were that ravished our sister.
For their fell faults our brothers were beheaded,

Our father's tears despis'd, and basely cozen'd

Can the son stand by and watch his father bleed?
Here's equal payment, death for death.

You sad faced men, people and sons of Rome,
torn apart by disturbances, like a flight of birds
scattered by winds and stormy gales,
let me show you how you can tie up
this scattered corn into one united sheaf,
build these broken limbs back into one healthy body;
otherwise Rome will turn on herself,
and the one to whom mighty kingdoms bow down,
like a desperate and shameful outcast,
will kill herself.
But if my grey hairs and wrinkled face,
witnesses of the experience of age,
cannot persuade you to listen to me,
[to Lucius] then speak, dear friend of Rome, as our
ancestor once
told lovesick Dido as she listened sadly

to his tale of that evil burning night
when the cunning Greeks ambushed King Priam's
Troy.
Tell us what Sinon has enchanted our ears,
or who brought the deadly machine in
that gives our Troy, our Rome, its internal wound.
My heart is not made of flint or steel;
nor can I tell all our bitter grief,
without floods of tears drowning my speech
and interrupting what I have to say, right at the time
when you should be listening to me most carefully,
and being most sympathetic.
Here's the young captain of Rome, let him tell the
tale,
while I stand by and weep to hear him speak.

Then, kind listeners, you should know
that Chiron and the cursed Demetrius
were the ones who murdered our Emperor's brother;
they were the ones who raped my sister.
For their dreadful crimes my brothers were
executed,
my father's tears were mocked, and he was cheaply

Of that true hand that fought Rome's quarrel out

And sent her enemies unto the grave.
Lastly, myself unkindly banished,
The gates shut on me, and turn'd weeping out,

To beg relief among Rome's enemies;
Who drown'd their enmity in my true tears,
And op'd their arms to embrace me as a friend.
I am the turned forth, be it known to you,
That have preserv'd her welfare in my blood
And from her bosom took the enemy's point,
Sheathing the steel in my advent'rous body.
Alas! you know I am no vaunter, I;
My scars can witness, dumb although they are,
That my report is just and full of truth.
But, soft! methinks I do digress too much,
Citing my worthless praise. O, pardon me!
For when no friends are by, men praise themselves.

tricked
into losing that loyal hand that fought in Rome's battles
and sent her enemies to the grave.
Lastly, I myself was unjustly exiled,
the gates were closed on me, I was turned out weeping,
to beg for help from the enemies of Rome;
they took pity and forgot their quarrels,
and opened their arms to embrace me as a friend.
You should know that I am the exile
that has kept Rome safe with my blood,
turning the enemy's sword away from her heart
and taking the steel in my own daring body.
Alas! You know I am no boaster;
my scars can witness, though they cannot speak,
that my story is right and true.
But, wait! I think I'm wandering from the point,
giving myself worthless praise. Excuse me!
When there are no friends around, men praise themselves.

MARCUS.
Now is my turn to speak. Behold the child.
[Pointing to the CHILD in an attendant's arms]
Of this was Tamora delivered,
The issue of an irreligious Moor,
Chief architect and plotter of these woes.
The villain is alive in Titus' house,
Damn'd as he is, to witness this is true.
Now judge what cause had Titus to revenge
These wrongs unspeakable, past patience,
Or more than any living man could bear.
Now have you heard the truth: what say you, Romans?
Have we done aught amiss, show us wherein,
And, from the place where you behold us pleading,
The poor remainder of Andronici
Will, hand in hand, all headlong hurl ourselves,
And on the ragged stones beat forth our souls,
And make a mutual closure of our house.
Speak, Romans, speak; and if you say we shall,
Lo, hand in hand, Lucius and I will fall.

Now it's my turn to speak. See the child.

Tamora gave birth to this,
fathered by an atheist Moor,
the main inspiration and plotter of these sorrows.
The villain is alive in Titus' house,
damned as he is, to witness the truth of this.
Now you must judge what right Titus had to revenge
these unspeakable wrongs, beyond endurance,
more than any mortal man could bear.
Now you've heard the truth; what do you say, Romans?
If we've done anything wrong, tell us what it is,
And the poor remains of the house of Andronicus
will all throw ourselves down, hand in hand,
from the place you can now see us speaking,
and smash out our souls on the jagged rocks,
and end our family for good.
Speak, Romans, speak; if you say we should,
then Lucius and I shall jump down, hand in hand.

AEMILIUS.
Come, come, thou reverend man of Rome,
And bring our Emperor gently in thy hand,
Lucius our Emperor; for well I know

Come, come, you respected Roman,
take our Emperor gently by the hand,
Lucius our Emperor; for I am certain

The common voice do cry it shall be so.

that the voice of the people say that's the case.

ALL.
Lucius, all hail, Rome's royal Emperor!

Lucius, praise you, the royal Emperor of Rome!

MARCUS.
Go, go into old Titus' sorrowful house,
And hither hale that misbelieving Moor
To be adjudg'd some direful slaught'ring death,
As punishment for his most wicked life.

Go into old Titus' sorrowful house,
and drag out that unbelieving Moor
to be sentenced to some horrible death
as punishment for his terrible wicked life.

Exeunt some attendants. LUCIUS, MARCUS, and the others descend

ALL.
Lucius, all hail, Rome's gracious governor!

Lucius, we salute you, Rome's gracious leader!

LUCIUS.
Thanks, gentle Romans! May I govern so
To heal Rome's harms and wipe away her woe!

Thanks, kind Romans! May I govern in a way
that heals Rome's wounds and wipes away her
sorrow!

But, gentle people, give me aim awhile,
For nature puts me to a heavy task.
Stand all aloof; but, uncle, draw you near

But, gentle people, watch me for a while,
as I perform the heavy task nature has given me.
Everyone stand back, except for you, uncle, come
near

To shed obsequious tears upon this trunk.
O, take this warm kiss on thy pale cold lips.
[Kisses TITUS]
These sorrowful drops upon thy blood-stain'd face,
The last true duties of thy noble son!

to shed funereal tears on this body.
Oh, take this warm kiss on your pale cold lips.

These sorrowful drops on your bloodstained face,
are the last duty your noble son can do for you.

MARCUS.
Tear for tear and loving kiss for kiss
Thy brother Marcus tenders on thy lips.
O, were the sum of these that I should pay
Countless and infinite, yet would I pay them!

Tear for tear and loving kiss for kiss
you brother Marcus places on your lips.
Oh, if the amount of these I should pay
was infinite, uncountable, I would still pay them.

LUCIUS.
Come hither, boy; come, come, come, and learn of us
To melt in showers. Thy grandsire lov'd thee well;

Come here boy, come, come, and learn from us
how to dissolve in tears. Your grandfather loved you
very much;

Many a time he danc'd thee on his knee,
Sung thee asleep, his loving breast thy pillow;

many times he dandled you on his knee,
and sang you to sleep, with his loving chest as your
pillow;

Many a story hath he told to thee,
And bid thee bear his pretty tales in mind
And talk of them when he was dead and gone.

he told you many stories,
and told you to keep his sweet tales in mind
and speak of them when he was dead and gone.

MARCUS.

How many thousand times hath these poor lips,
When they were living, warm'd themselves on thine!
O, now, sweet boy, give them their latest kiss!
Bid him farewell; commit him to the grave;
Do them that kindness, and take leave of them.

BOY.
O grandsire, grandsire! ev'n with all my heart

Would I were dead, so you did live again!
O Lord, I cannot speak to him for weeping;
My tears will choke me, if I ope my mouth.
Re-enter attendants with AARON

A ROMAN.
You sad Andronici, have done with woes;
Give sentence on the execrable wretch
That hath been breeder of these dire events.

LUCIUS.
Set him breast-deep in earth, and famish him;

There let him stand and rave and cry for food.
If any one relieves or pities him,
For the offence he dies. This is our doom.
Some stay to see him fast'ned in the earth.

AARON.
Ah, why should wrath be mute and fury dumb?

I am no baby, I, that with base prayers
I should repent the evils I have done;
Ten thousand worse than ever yet I did
Would I perform, if I might have my will.
If one good deed in all my life I did,
I do repent it from my very soul.

LUCIUS.
Some loving friends convey the Emperor hence,
And give him burial in his father's grave.
My father and Lavinia shall forthwith
Be closed in our household's monument.
As for that ravenous tiger, Tamora,
No funeral rite, nor man in mourning weed,
No mournful bell shall ring her burial;
But throw her forth to beasts and birds to prey.

---

*How many thousands of times have these poor lips,
when they were alive, warmed themselves on yours!
Oh now, sweet boy, give them their last kiss!
Say goodbye to him; send him to his grave;
do this kindness, and then leave them.*

*Oh grandfather, grandfather! I wish with all my heart
that I were dead, if it meant you would live again!
Oh Lord, I cannot speak to him for weeping;
my tears will choke me, if I open my mouth.*

*You sad Andronici, finish with your sorrows;
pass sentence on the horrible wretch
that inspired these terrible events.*

*Bury him up to the chest in the earth, and starve him;
let him stand there and rave and cry for food.
If anyone helps or pities him
they shall die for it. This is my sentence.
Some of you stop here and make sure he is buried in the earth.*

*Ah, why should my anger be quiet and my fury silent?
I am not some baby who will with groveling prayers
repent all the evils I have done;
If I had my way I'd do ten thousand more,
all worse than the ones I've already done.
If I ever did one good thing in my life
I'm sorry for it from the bottom of my soul.*

*Some loving friends carry the Emperor away,
and bury him in his father's grave.
My father and Lavinia shall be put at once
in our family mausoleum.
As for that vicious tiger, Tamora,
she shall have no funeral rites, no mourners,
no sad bell will toll for her burial;
throw her out to the animals and the birds of prey.*

Her life was beastly and devoid of pity,
And being dead, let birds on her take pity.

Exeunt

Her life was beastly and empty of pity,
so now she's dead, let the birds take pity on her.

15199058R00060